FOREWORD BY MARIO MURILLO

A NEW ERA FOR AMERICA,
THE CHURCH, AND THE NATIONS

THE
TUMULTUOUS
2020s
AND BEYOND

BERT M. FARIAS

The Tumultuous 2020's and Beyond
Copyright © 2019
Bert M. Farias
Cover design by Lisa Hainline, LionsGate Media

A Holy Fire Ministry Publication.
Printed in the United States of America.
ISBN-13: 978-0-578-62331-3

Library of Congress data is available for this title.

CONTENTS

FOREWORD BY MARIO MURILLO

Warnings from God carry only two potential outcomes. The first is a profound gratitude when certain disaster is averted. The other is unbridled remorse for ignoring the warning.

Today, warnings from God must navigate a minefield of cheap grace, false hope, and arrogance. Too many preachers today sound the same — many even have the same inflections in their voice. They are dancing before the Body of Christ with false comfort every bit as much as the seduced prophets danced before Ahab in 1 Kings 22.

In the midst of that, Micaiah the prophet—who suffered the greatest pressure ever to conform and sound like everybody else—reacted with one of the most courageous phrases in history. *"As the Lord lives, I will speak what the Lord says to me"* (1 Kings 22:14).

We must never look at circumstances. We must see through them. Once you see through them you must see past them. You can only do this with warnings that come by God's Spirit.

THE TUMULTUOUS 2020'S AND BEYOND by BERT M. FARIAS is a warning from God to protect you in the coming days. Bert says what the Lord told him to say, and he does not care about the consequences. The 2020s will be the greatest test American believers have ever faced.

Never forget that God-given warnings are sent out of love — not out of anger, or hate. This book is a Godsend to help you not only face the 2020s but to thrive for God in them.

It is my sincere prayer that God will turn this much needed warning into a much heeded warning.

ENDORSEMENTS

The ministry of Bert Farias is marked by the burning heart of a prophet and the anointed passion of a revivalist. I believe he is a voice that God has raised up in this hour with an important message for the church. In Bert's newest work — *The Tumultuous 2020s and Beyond* — the clarion call that characterizes his ministry comes through with a cutting edge that is sharp and clear. In this timely book, Bert Farias pulls no punches as he tackles relevant and controversial issues that will define the Church in our generation and determine what we pass on to the next. I highly recommend Bert Farias, his ministry, and this book.

Daniel Kolenda

President and CEO, Christ for the Nations

The Tumultuous 2020's and Beyond is a clarion call to the body of Christ to return to its first love, but with a warning: It will challenge you to examine what you believe and why; it may even make you angry at times. Bert effectively lays out the sad state of politics, morals, agendas, and problems of our day, and then, while clearly laying out the consequences of continuing along the current path, he presents the solution. This book is prophetic, quoting several prophecies and inspired words on what is to come in the natural world, while at the same time showing the glory of the body of Christ rising up to fulfill her destiny. A must-read!

John Fenn

Founder, Church Without Walls International

This book by Bert Farias is like fine wine. God has truly reserved some of the best and most authentic oracles for these last days. With urgency and a father's heart, Bert ushers the reader into a tremendous vision of the future and a clear call to repentance and sobriety. If you are ready for a serious burden from heaven and possess a desire to impact the world around you, start reading now!

Jeremiah Johnson

Best Selling Author and Founder of Heart of the Father Ministry

OTHER BOOKS BY BERT M. FARIAS

I'm not so sure, if Jesus should tarry, that these books won't still be read a century from now. They are timeless truths for the depraved day we are living in, they have a deep sanctifying effect on the inward man, and they serve as a plumb line to avoid the same repeated spiritual errors in every generation. These truly are books for the end of days.

SOULISH LEADERSHIP

PURITY OF HEART

THE JOURNAL OF A JOURNEY TO HIS HOLINESS

THE REAL SPIRIT OF REVIVAL

THE REAL SALVATION

THE REAL GOSPEL

THE REAL JESUS

MY SON, MY SON: FATHERING AND TRAINING A HOLY GENERATION (A parenting book)

PRAYER: THE LANGUAGE OF THE SPIRIT

PASSING ON THE MOVE OF GOD TO THE NEXT GENERA-TION

CLEANSING THE TEMPLE: RESTORING THE GLORY OF THE LORD

*To order any of these books, visit our website,

(www.holy-fire.org), or Amazon books.*

If this book or any of Bert's other books have been a blessing to you, kindly post a review on Amazon.

INTRODUCTION

For more than two centuries the United States of America has been one of the most prosperous and powerful nations of the world. Its military power and its economic superiority actually holds the world together. If the U.S. crumbled or imploded, China would take over the whole of the Far East. Pakistan and India would more than likely break out in war, as both possess nuclear weapons. Iran would cause unlimited chaos and madness in the Middle East. These are just a few examples of what could happen.

But slowly and gradually in recent years, America's moral high ground, which caused God to mercifully protect this land, has begun a downward slide. Then, during the last decade, we've witnessed the nation spiraling into an abyss. Her enemies within sprang up in our marketplaces, court systems, universities, in the high and low places of our government, and, of course, in the unprincipled, mad, lying media.

I believe you will be greatly enlightened from my findings in Chapter 5 of this book that there are also now many enemies within various branches and large segments of the Church itself. An all-out hellish assault has been doubly unleashed to lull the Church to sleep, render her ineffective, and crush and destroy our nation.

Islamists, atheists, LGBT, Planned Parenthood, activist judges, and a president who embraced an anti-biblical, one-world ideology dominated American culture in the last decade. Hollywood also aided in spearheading this evil, violence, and corruption throughout the world.

During these turbulent times, born again Christians and Messianic Jews began to pray. Thank God that across the nation there were enough saints who saw what was happening and began to cry out to

God. Prayer movements for true revival and awakening intensified among the remnant people of God.

God's response was to miraculously allow an unlikely business-man, Donald J. Trump, to be elected to the presidency of the United States of America. God foresaw that this hot-blooded and temperamental man would have the backbone and character to stand up against the hordes of demonic forces that were intent on destroying our nation. Now these forces, working through unregenerate, wicked, and unreasonable men, are moving in chaotic desperation as they witness President Donald Trump undoing the work of the last president and gaining momentum for a second-term run.

Contrariwise, some of Obama's last acts as he left the presidency were: (1) to free a homosexual spy from prison, (2) to allow his Department of Justice and the FBI, buried deep in corruption under his administration, to spy on the opposing presidential candidate, and (3) to purposely refuse to use his veto power in the Security Council, leaving Israel with a UN resolution that states that Israeli towns and communities in Judea and Samaria are in "flagrant violation" of international law.

This resolution has given a great boost to the Boycott, Divestment, and Sanctions Movement, with the goal of destroying Israel's economy. This resolution also means that the Old City of Jerusalem and the Mount of Olives does not belong to Israel, as far as the UN is concerned (see below).

Today President Trump is working to protect Christians whose faith is being attacked by atheistic judges. He is working against a One World open border and denying the Democrats their dream of allowing literally millions of foreigners into America, and to carry out unlawful deeds such as granting illegal immigrants free medical services, free schooling, and free housing, as well as voter rights to everyone with no citizenship or even identification.

And certainly one of President Trump's greatest achievements has been to confirm, at the time of this writing, 170 new conservative judges in our nation.

I must honestly say: I cannot imagine how any true Christian or Messianic Jew can be a Democrat today. It is quickly morphing into a Marxist, socialist, violently atheistic party with great greed for power. One cannot read his Bible and be a leftist liberal democrat. You have to feed on humanistic ideologies and go to humanistic schools to be one.

As for Israel, right now God is using President Trump and his close associates as a huge shield to the nation of Israel. He has done more for Israel in such a short time than anyone could have imagined. According to polls, he is more popular in Israel than in any other nation in the world. Right now he is also moving quickly to protect the Christians in America and in other nations as well.

The Democrats will do everything in their power to defeat the president and vote in a 2020 president who will free up Planned Parenthood and continue to increase the murder of the unborn. They will try to fully restore the forced brainwashing of nursery and school children to believe and accept the false happiness of being a transgender and to get used to seeing men in the girls' bathroom. These are the facts. Much of our educational system, from nursery school children to our university levels, is now a sewer of anti-Christ, antisemite, and humanistic beliefs.

Some of you may not know it, but Israel imitates America. Lots of nations follow America. But we also cannot forget for one minute that

God has promised that all of Israel shall be saved, and He has promised to pour out His Spirit on all flesh.

Finally, God has allowed a great divide between the right and the left wings of our government. No one who says he serves Jesus Christ and who reads his Bible will have any excuse for not knowing what is good and righteous and what is evil and wicked in this hour. It is becoming increasingly clear in these tumultuous times what is light and what is darkness, and what is Biblical morality and what is violent, intolerant Marxist socialism.

So if we care about this land from sea to shining sea, we will pray unceasingly that in our lifetime and the lifetimes of our children and grandchildren and future generations, God will keep godly men and women in office, and cleanse and strengthen the Church, so that America can continue to be a shining light to the world; we must pray that the works of Satan will be defeated in America, especially in this next election. This is a season of reprieve and opportunity — all so we can buy more time to right the ship and rewrite the script for the Church and the nation.

"*Therefore I exhort first of all that supplications, prayers, intercessions, and giving of thanks be made for all men, for kings and all who are in authority, that we may lead a quiet and peaceable life in all godliness and reverence. For this is good and acceptable in the sight of God our Savior, who desires all men to be saved and to come to the knowledge of the truth*" (1 Tim. 2:1-4).

Notice the connection between praying for governmental leaders and the salvation of men's souls. When a nation legislates and restricts the propagation of the gospel, it becomes more difficult for the people of that nation to hear the gospel and be saved. In America, not only have we enjoyed these liberties, but the gospel has been carried from this nation to the entire world. This is probably the biggest reason and God's greatest purpose in keeping America free from its anti-Christ enemies and preserving her "one nation under God" sovereignty.

PRAYER: Lord, we pray continually that You will hear our prayers, and that You will grant mercy for America. We pray that You will pour out Your Spirit on Your mighty remnant, who are advancing Your kingdom and fighting the good fight of faith for the salvation of souls and for the saving and sovereignty of our nation. Amen.

***According to Wikipedia, the Boycott, Divestment and Sanctions movement (also known as BDS) is a Palestinian-led campaign promoting various forms of boycott against Israel until it meets what the campaign describes as Israel's obligations under international law, defined as withdrawal from the occupied territories, removal of the separation barrier in the West Bank, full equality for Arab-Palestinian citizens of Israel, and "respecting, protecting, and promoting the rights of Palestinian refugees to return to their homes and properties." The campaign is organized and coordinated by the Palestinian BDS National Committee.

As this book was going to print the headlines reported this good news:

Secretary of State Mike Pompeo said that the United States will no longer consider Israeli settlements to be illegal under international law, a move that formalizes the Trump administration's treatment of the West Bank and shifts decades of U.S. policy. If true and accurate, this report means that U.S. policy is now in line with the revealed will of God. We are living in the time when God is bringing home the Jews and restoring their Promised Land just as He said He would (Ezekiel 36 and 37 and Jeremiah chapters 30 and 31).

This announcement, which could not have happened without President Trump's approval, places America even more solidly in compliance with this accurate translation of Gen. 12:3:

"And all the families of the earth shall bless themselves by you."

America has blessed themselves by aligning with God's will for Israel.

CHAPTER 1

"2020 will be a year when the nation will be totally divided. It will be the year that will see the election of your lifetime." — Mario Murillo

I have said it for years. The Bible confirms it. Bittersweet times are ahead. The darkness will get darker. The light will grow brighter. The distinction between the righteous and unrighteous, the true Church and the carnal, compromising church will be much more visible. God has allowed the wheat and tares to grow up together and both shall reach maturity during the final ingathering of souls.

In many ways the decade of the 2020s will be the most tumultuous decade in American history. Take a look at this definition of tumultuous: *making a loud, confused noise; uproarious.*

Now read these next definitions slowly, while thinking of the recent 2016 elections, up till now:

Loud, deafening, thunderous, thundering, ear-shattering, earsplitting, ear-piercing, uproarious, noisy, clamorous, vociferous, excited, confused, or disorderly.

Here are some more synonyms to describe tumultuous: *tempestuous, stormy, turbulent, in turmoil, passionate, intense, explosive, violent, volatile, and full of upheavals.*

Are you getting the picture? If what many of us are sensing is true, we are in for a wild roller coaster ride of a lifetime. I sincerely believe this is the finest hour for the rising remnant people of God, but not so for those in disagreement with God.

THE PRE-ELECTION CONSPIRACY ESSAY AND THE HEAD-ON COLLISION WITH THE GLOBAL LIBERAL SWAMP

A conspiracy essay was written in 2015 concerning a possible Donald Trump presidency. I wondered why no one took credit for the article. To this day, no one really knows who wrote it. Here is what the article said:

"They will kill him before they let him be president. It could be a Republican or a Democrat that instigates the shutting up of Trump. Don't be surprised if Trump has an accident. Some people are getting very nervous: Barack Obama, Valerie Jarrett, Eric Holder, Hillary Clinton, and Jon Corzine, to name just a few. It's about the unholy dynamics between big government, big business, and big media. They all benefit by the billions of dollars from this partnership, and it's in all of their interests to protect one another. It's one for all and all for one.

"It's a heck of a filthy relationship that makes everyone filthy rich, everyone except the American people. We get ripped off. We're the patsies. But for once, the powerful socialist cabal and the corrupt crony capitalists are scared. The over-the-top reaction to Trump by politicians of both parties, the media, and the biggest corporations of America has been so swift and insanely angry that it suggests they are all threatened and frightened like never before.

"Donald Trump can self-fund. No matter how much they say to the contrary, the media, business, and political elite understand that Trump is no joke. He could actually win and upset their nice, cozy apple cart.

"It's no coincidence that everyone has gotten together to destroy The Donald. It's because most of the other politicians are

part of the good-old-boys club. They talk big, but they won't change a thing. They are all beholden to big-money donors. They are all owned by lobbyists, unions, lawyers, gigantic environmental organizations, and multinational corporations ... like Big Pharma or Big Oil."

How mysteriously accurate this article was when the odds of a Donald Trump presidency were still very remote! Thank God he has not been assassinated. He needs our prayers now more than ever. At this writing he is 73 years old, and the pressure of a second term will be immense and could take a toll on his aging body and mind.

Can you see the miracle his election was? And while Trump is not the savior of our country in the spiritual sense, he is the beginning of a miracle for the Church. I see him as a sort of gatekeeper, keeping America from a stay of execution. As I heard one national voice say, he is an act of God to buy the Church time to repent and return to her rightful role in American life. No, Trump is not a pastor or a moral reformer, but he is clearly an instrument of restraint to a full-blown national political, moral, and spiritual disaster. If the Church doesn't seize the time and opportunity God has opened, disaster will strike on America like a serpent's head.

WHAT THE CHURCH MUST DO

God has a divine response to every demonic plan. Since the days of Christ's crucifixion and glorious resurrection, the devil is the ultimate symbol of defeat. He is only a puppet to those who are *not* ignorant of his devices. It is only through the weapon of deceit that he holds the world in bondage. We who know his true state continually exercise our authority over him. This marks one of the chief differences between the true Church and the carnal, compromising church in this hour.

Believers must maintain two positions in this hour: Lay low before the Lord in consecration and prayer, and stand up against the forces of darkness in the authority of Jesus Christ.

1. **The first order for the Church is to be in agreement with God.** Sadly, many professing believers are on the devil's side. You cannot walk in the authority of Christ if you're living in sin and walking in darkness and in Satanic ideologies. Remember that a house or a kingdom divided against itself will not stand (Matt. 12:25-30). The Church cannot tacitly approve abortion, same sex marriage, and remain silent against all the evils that have infiltrated and are now dominating American culture. We cannot ignore and live in the politically correct zone concerning the dangers of radical Islam and the anti-Christ agenda in America. Silence in such an evil day is grief to the Holy Spirit and a certain impending judgment.

2. **The second order for the Church must be to forsake church growth-ism and popularity, and actually restore and nurture kingdom culture.** Simply put, attendance on Sunday morning is great, but the kingdom encompasses a lifestyle. The awakened Church is transitioning from an image-based, consumer-driven enterprise to a relationship-based family, and kingdom-consumed army. What this means is not only receiving people into our church buildings but receiving them into our hearts, our lives, and homes. This will cost us our very lives, but joy and peace will fill our hearts as we labor in the harvest fields of humanity.

3. **Thirdly, the commitment to love and unity and the increase of the manifestation of the supernatural power of God will catapult the Church into far greater effectiveness and fruitfulness in the coming decade.** Believers will learn to

live a Spirit-filled life, and a holy love and devotion to one another will mark their walk with God. I am seeing this love and honor growing among the remnant wherever I go. Ministers are preferring one another before themselves. Local shepherds are reaching out to other local shepherds and cultivating relationship and prayer with them. Believers who are dissatisfied with the world, and carnal, compromising church systems are banding and bonding together. This is actually a move of the Spirit that will quietly mushroom and affect entire economies as this unity prevails. The true Church will be a place of refuge for multitudes who will find true peace and fulfillment within its embrace.

God is preparing and positioning us for great battles and great victories in the tumultuous 2020s. We are now in a precursor time of repentance, judgment, and cleansing (refer to my book, *Cleansing the Temple*).

Due to the diverse nature of the Church she will continue to take on many forms and structures, and the Lord will use and bless each as much as He can, because He loves people. But the awakened, rising remnant and those who truly know their covenant-keeping God will do exploits (Dan. 11:32).

CHAPTER 2

TIME FOR AUTHENTIC CHRISTIANITY DEVOID OF MIXTURE

The great American revivalist Charles Finney once said that the character of the age is changing and that the Church and its preachers must adapt. Many of our church leaders have recognized this — specifically that 21st century living is complex and more demanding, with most people's lives being a constant whirlwind of activity, their minds bombarded with technology and information, their spirits numbed by social media and many other distractions. Because many are incapable of properly managing and balancing their lives, they grow tired, exhausted, and in many ways, they feel isolated and craving genuine relationships. Depression has been the result and is plaguing more people now than perhaps at any other time in history.

Strong preaching and the demands of the gospel are like fingernails on a chalkboard to some. Has the Church adapted? Yes, but the problem has been that the adaptation that many preachers and churches have made has come with many unhealthy compromises.

So, to get converts and church members we've toned down on holiness, the requirements of discipleship, and sound doctrine, and offered people a cheap-grace-and-sloppy-love gospel while almost nullifying the necessity of the demonstration of the Spirit and power of God. Thus, the so-called "progressive" church has been birthed. Its hybrid twin, the "seeker-friendly" church, was also birthed. This church model has done more damage and highjacked more truth in a shorter amount of time than in any other period in American history (refer to author's book, *Passing on the Move of God to the Next Generation*). That's why I agree with the following quote:

"The American church is guilty of great crimes against the Holy Spirit. We told Him to leave and let us grow "Christianity Incorporated" — the worst thing we could have done. It was a mistake — a terrible, incalculable, ongoing mistake — derailing more truth in less time than any moral plague in history." — Mario Murillo

Not only have we told the Holy Spirit to leave, but as I said, the Word of God has been greatly compromised and even corrupted. It has been my observation in these progressive churches where liberal theology has infiltrated that, not only has there been a diminished respect for the Bible, but even foundational Christian doctrine is questioned and challenged. The erosion of the most basic tenets of the faith is appalling in some denominational and mainline churches.

For example, some no longer even believe that Jesus Christ is the only way to salvation, but that there are many ways and religions that lead to God. No joke. Some no longer believe that the Bible is the fully inspired word of God, but rather a book written or tampered with by men (see my book, *The Real Salvation*) (Barna survey).

I know this sounds extreme and hard to believe for the P/C (Pentecostal/Charismatic) people, but we must understand that the term "Christian" no longer encompasses what is basic to foundational Christian doctrine. To be a "Christian" in America has a much broader scope of meaning than it had before among the hundreds of thousands of churches that dot our landscape. Even globally, that is so. "Disciple" or "disciplined follower of Jesus" should be the new word to describe a real 21st-century Christian.

THE UNHOLY MIXTURE

This girl followed Paul and us, and cried out, saying, "These men are the servants of the Most High God, who proclaim to us the way of salvation" (Acts 16:17).

23

In the above verse, when Satan used a slave girl possessed with a spirit of divination to identify herself and her fortune telling with Paul's team, it was his master plan to defile the church of God with other mixtures. He has done this successfully throughout the ages. It's always been his lethal stroke. "If you can't beat 'em, join 'em" is the devil's mode of operation. Throughout history and increasingly so today, Christianity is a myriad of traditions, doctrines of demons, witchcraft, and now New Age gobbledygook. Unfortunately, some of this mixture has also infiltrated into the Pentecostal/Charismatic camp.

Listen carefully to some of today's most popular teachers. They are popular because most of what they teach is ear tickling, pleasant, affirming, and non-confrontational. For the most part, it's a happiness/prosperity gospel. It certainly does not contain any power to get you beaten and thrown in jail. The whole counsel of God is missing from their presentation. In many cases, opinions and feelings are emphasized more than the Scriptures. These teachers and pastors are a part of what I call "progressive" and "seeker-friendly" churches that really are digressive. In many of them, sin and redemption have been exchanged for social justice and doing good.

Multitudes of people have hidden themselves behind these fig-leaf churches. They are content in being religious. The fig leafs are their self-righteous works and the natural goodness of a person, but according to Finney, they are useless for revival.

"There is a certain type of Christian that although being constructively involved in the church and pass off as being very good Christians are useless in revival. I do not mean that they are wicked, but they have a form of piety which has no fire and efficiency and actually repels new believers, and wards off the truth."

24

The social and economic pressure in our Western culture is greater than it's ever been. The decade of the 2020s will be filled with increasingly stressful situations in our nation, more natural disasters, some that may greatly alter the socio-economic structure of the nation, and the pace of life will not get any slower. The seeds of Marxist socialism, Islam, and atheistic communism have been sown in America, and the jury is still out as to what kind of harvest they will produce. The indoctrination of an anti-Christ agenda has gained momentum in the last generation. But GOD!

Here's what I believe and see coming: All of these characteristics of a humanistic new age will result in more and more people connecting with the emptiness of their own hearts. This will result in multitudes sensing their need for the reality of the living God and the peace and joy that comes from Jesus, even in the midst of chaos, hatred, and unrest. There is a great harvest of souls coming, and we must be ready.

CHAPTER 3

SAVE THE CHURCH, SAVE THE NATION

Dutch Sheets said this in a recent article:

"A demonic tide of destruction has been unleashed upon our nation, and is taking ground at an increasingly rapid rate. Politically, economically, and humanistically, there is an agenda to make this nation never again look the way it has looked before. Yet God has not given up on America! He has a great plan and a purpose for this nation, and He is calling on us to partner with His heart and His strategy in this critical hour."

Here is a quote from America's founding fathers, who made a covenant with God:

"We do hereby dedicate this land to raise up godly generations. May this covenant of dedication remain unto all generations. May all who see this cross remember what we have done here, and may those who come here to inhabit join us in this new covenant."

The effects of that covenant are still operative.

Sheets went on to compare the days we are living in to the days of Ezra, and how in response to people's hunger and desperation God raised up a company of leaders, among them, Haggai and Zecharias, two prophets, along with Joshua the high priest (representing God's government), and Zerubbabel the governor (representing civil government), and how they joined together to lead the people into reformation. All of them worked in agreement to move God's people toward repentance and the restoration of the temple (again, please refer to my book *Cleansing the Temple,* to discover the depth of purification and

26

consecration that must happen to restore the glory of the Lord in His people). This is exactly where we are as a Church and a nation going into the 2020s.

The most exciting part of this account in Ezra is that in response to their obedience and righteous partnership, the Lord blessed them by decreeing that the glory of the latter house would be greater than the former (Hag. 2:9). This is my hope for the Church and the nation.

Notice how the prophets, the high priest, and the governor worked together to lead the people into reformation (Hag. 1:1). This pattern and type and shadow is seen throughout the Old Testament. In God's kingdom there is no separation of Church and state. We are to take the kingdom into every facet of society. When bad things happen in our country, often the Church is to blame. Lack of watchfulness, prayerfulness, and obedience to God creates a vacuum for Satan to fill. When Obama, an enemy of the state, in my humble opinion, was elected president, the Church was to blame. I know that statement will not win me more friends, but I will keep saying it. Millions of "Christians" voted for the most anti-Biblical president in American history. It was an issue of very poor stewardship.

We are in the mess we're in now because too many professing Christians voted foolishly or didn't vote at all. Hilton Sutton, the prophecy teacher, who is now with the Lord, conducted altar calls of repentance near the end of his life for Christians who had voted for Obama. Even now, so many professing "Christians" have sided in with the corrupt, ungodly media and have been brainwashed to hate President Trump, who has helped the Church's cause perhaps more than any president in American history. Professing "Christians" need to either discern and vote for righteousness and Biblical values or quit calling themselves Christians.

"*The time has come that Christians must vote for honest men and take consistent ground in politics or the Lord will curse them. Christians seem to act as if they thought God did not see what they do in politics. But I tell you He does see it, and He will bless or curse this nation according to the course the Christians take in politics.*"— Charles G. Finney

Those are strong words, and you may not agree with them. You just watch. All hell will break loose in the next election. Refer to the conspiracy essay against Trump before his presidency that I referred to in the first chapter. Barring a miracle, expect much more of that.

VERY SERIOUS TIMES

I must say this again. We are in a very serious time of judgment and cleansing right now. There are two cleansings in the ministry of Jesus. He cleansed the temple at the beginning (Jn. 2) and at the end of His public ministry (Mt. 21, Mk. 11, Lk. 19). In the end, this cleansing prepared the way for a new order that His resurrection and ascension would bring.

The Church is coming into a new order and will look vastly different than it has in recent times. Church leaders and ministers must be open to this change that is coming with both new wine and a new wineskin that will foreseeably evolve in times of persecution. There must be a cleansing so that the Lord's glory can be restored in His people before the worst shall come. America is on the brink of judgment, and we must judge ourselves, so that when judgment falls on the world, the Church will be separate, and her impact will be greater. I don't know about you, but as a minister, I'm making more heart-felt adjustments and continual changes in my own life. I want to love and fear God more.

We need to heed Stanley Frodsham's prophetic words for we are nearer to their fulfillment than when he first spoke them in 1965.

"With great judgments will I plead with the population of this country. Great darkness is coming upon the countries that have heard My gospel but no longer walk in it. My wrath shall come upon them."

And then he prophesied this:

"Before I visit the nations in judgment; I will begin at My house. When I do cause My wrath to come upon the cities of the world, My people shall be separate. I desire a people without spot or wrinkle, and such will be preserved by Me in the time of My wrath, which will be coming upon all iniquity and unrighteousness."

IS YOUR CHURCH FLIRTING WITH DELILAH?

Is your church a happy church ... one that doesn't make you feel uncomfortable ... one that will never offend you ... one that will always tell you how much they love you and how much God loves you?

Marketing-based leaders change their church name for branding an image. They change their church culture for wooing the masses. They assemble cool young bands that play cool, uplifting music and songs. They adapt their message for itching ears and unknowingly take away the power of redemption.

What I have just described is the current trend of many churches.

The happy church will entertain you. They say they exist to give people hope. They have fun programs for all your children. All their music and songs will make you feel special and soothe your guilt-ridden emotions. And they'll do whatever they can to keep you coming back for more.

This is the church that is flirting with Delilah. If they stay there too long, their conscience will be seared, and they will be prime targets for deception and destruction. They won't be able to shake themselves free, because they won't know that the anointing has departed from them.

Delilah lulled Samson to sleep on her knees and called for a man to shave off the seven locks of his hair. Then she began to humiliate him, and his strength left him.

She said, "*The Philistines are upon you, Samson.*"

Then he awakened from his sleep and said, "*I will go out as before and shake myself free." But he did not know that the Lord had left him* (Judges 16:19-20).

Samson flirted with Delilah until the secret of his power was cut off. Like so many churches and leaders today, he didn't realize he had lost the anointing until it was too late. The secret of Samson's power was his long hair. The secret of the church's power is the mighty Holy Spirit.

Delilah bewitched Samson. Popular voices and popular concepts are bewitching today's church.

"*O foolish Galatians! Who has bewitched you that you should not obey the truth? ... Are you so foolish? Having begun in the Spirit, are you now being perfected by the flesh?" Gal.* 3:1, 3).

A DISTURBING DREAM

A disturbing dream was given to my wife. She was driving to a church service amidst great devastation. Roads had been damaged. Cars blown up. Trees were down. Destruction was all around. As she approached the front door of where the church was meeting, the door-keeper directed her to enter another way.

She had to walk behind the venue and crawl through a low porch window. Once inside, my wife saw carpenters working, people smoking and swearing, coarse conversations, and tales of adultery. Farther below, she entered the room where people gathered. In the dream, I got up to preach, burning with the fire of holiness, and immediately, an assassination attempt was made on me by an instrument that shot out strange fire.

Then, on the way home from that meeting, my wife ran into a very weary and spiritually depleted member of this church, who was being affected by the deadness of this once life-giving church.

Just as there are evil alliances in the world, so there are in the church. Both are subtle. Both are demonic. We wrestle not against flesh and blood. They are seducing spirits promoting doctrines of demons. It's rampant and worse than many think. Nice people who have been deceived are engaged and involved in these unholy alliances.

THE TITANIC IS SINKING, BUT WE'RE STILL PLAYING

The *Titanic* is sinking, but the band keeps playing, and the singers keep singing. Warnings have been issued of the impending danger and devastation. The ark is being built, as in the days of Noah, but people are going about their business with great indifference and unbelief.

When people are about to drown and die, you don't plan parties. You don't entertain the masses. You don't need to hear monotone voices telling you everything is all right. That's cruel. It's like telling a lost sinner on his deathbed that everything's going to be all right when he's about to split hell wide open.

It's telling church goers that homosexuality is all right—that eventually, everyone goes to heaven, that there is no hell. It's dumbing down on the vital necessity of the baptism of the Holy Spirit and the power of God. It's remaining silent about controversial issues that affect the church while laws and legislation continue to be passed to rob us of more of our liberties. How can we keep silent during such an onslaught of evil on the Church and our nation? Cultural conditions have been changing for a number of years now, and with it, the rules have also changed.

A demonic culture with unimaginable addictions needs to meet a Church and a people full of power and unapologetic fire. In a time of mass murders in public gatherings and in the halls of our schools and churches — in a time of hurricanes, earthquakes, floods, and fires, and volcanoes on the brink of deathly eruptions — we don't want to see Noah swinging his hips from the platform of the ark and telling you how wonderful you are and how God will make all your dreams come true. It is not a time for pastors to display their wealth, talk of their multi-million-dollar airplanes, and grant people mild cures for their life-threatening diseases and lustful addictions.

I don't care how large your church is if it is not a threat to Satan's kingdom and the encompassing darkness. I don't care how popular a speaker you are if hell doesn't know you. If all people do is sing your praises, God hasn't sent you. If you only make people glad, but never sad or mad, you're probably doing a bad job. It means you're not impacting the culture of sin. In fact, worse than that, you're inoculating your own people against the real Jesus, the real gospel, and the real salvation (see my three books that bear these titles).

If you're in a happy church where the cross, the blood, and hell are never preached, where there's no real power to redeem from sin, and no warnings are ever given, you might be flirting with Delilah. You had better exit now, before your strength is cut off.

CHAPTER 4

THE COUNTERCULTURE CHURCH CANNOT CO-EXIST

In spite of church growth-ism in America…in spite of the greatest number of megachurches in our history…in spite of many seemingly successful Christian enterprises…in spite of pastors boasting of their supposed impact…we are experiencing the most rapid moral decline in America's history.

Atheism and heathenism have accelerated. Our public school system and universities are mass-producing socialists, communists, and those with an aggressive anti-Christ agenda. And get this: nearly half of all millennial Christians now believe evangelism is wrong. Hard to believe that one, but those Barna surveys are fairly accurate.

Driven by a lust for popularity, position, and power, many church pastors and leaders have wantonly turned a deaf ear to this national disaster that has dismantled faith and morality in America. It is a terrible thing to think that much of what we call "Christianity" in our land has become a system devoid of the reality and power that marked its earliest beginnings.

In a majority of our churches, tradition, formality, entertainment and social justice have actually made their version of "Christianity" perhaps the greatest enemy of the cause of Christ—a bastion of order, technique, form, and philosophy that has ironically served to immunize us against the real Christ and the real gospel. Probably the worst of it is that we've become a consumer-driven and image-based enterprise that has left off the real demands of Christ and the call to genuine discipleship that makes us all fishers of men.

Listen to the words of Eugene Peterson:

'*A huge religious marketplace has been set up in North America to meet the needs and fantasies of people just like us. There are conferences and gatherings custom-designed to give us what we need. Books and videos and seminars promise to let us in on the Christian "secret" of whatever we feel is lacking in our life: Financial security, well-behaved children, weight loss, exotic sex, travel to holy sites, exciting worship, and celebrity teachers. The people who promote these goods and services all smile a lot and are good looking.*

"We have become consumers of packaged spiritualities. This is idolatry. We never think of using this term for it, since everything we are buying or paying for is defined by the adjective "Christian." But idolatry it is, nevertheless: God packaged as a product; God depersonalized and made available as a technique or program. The Christian market in idols has never been more brisk or lucrative."

HERE'S THE GOOD NEWS

As men and women, young and old, are becoming more and more dissatisfied with the systems of this world and with the American gospel enterprise version of Christianity, we are now seeing a remnant of true God-seekers and leaders who actually pray and fast, and are passionate lovers of Jesus who will not compromise the gospel and resort to slick marketing to draw the attention of society. They are preaching the offense of the cross of Christ, not with enticing words of man's speech but in demonstration of the Spirit and power of God (1 Cor. 2:4-5). They are trusting the Holy Spirit to direct and build the church. We are now seeing a growing number of these messengers and God-men on the scene, and more are coming. It is a countercultural Christianity that will be contagious and spread like wildfire among those who long for real meaning and purpose in life. These are the Jesus people, the Jesus lovers.

This will result in a collision with consumerism Christianity that's based on compromise and flows with the culture. There will be a mass exodus from so-called "progressive" and "seeker-friendly" churches, and a great harvest of prodigals and false converts will be restored and genuinely converted. It will upset the religious crowd and much of our humanistic American culture. The two shall no longer coexist. There will be uprisings. There will be riots. There will be increased persecution of the righteous. But there will also be revivals and explosions of zeal witnessed in fiery new converts.

Everything that can be shaken will be shaken. It's not too late. In fact, it's just beginning.

CHAPTER 5

THE CORRUPTION OF AMERICAN CHRISTIANITY

AND THE EVIL AGENDA TO DESTROY AMERICA

"Now the Spirit clearly says that in the last times some will depart from the faith and pay attention to seducing spirits and doctrines of devils" (1 Tim. 4:1).

"Preach the word, be ready in season and out of season, reprove, rebuke, and exhort, with all patience and teaching. For the time will come when people will not endure sound doctrine, but they will gather to themselves teachers in accordance with their own desires, having itching ears" (2 Tim. 4:2-3).

A subversive effort by the leftist-leaning liberals to infiltrate the Church and turn people away from the real gospel and true doctrine is gaining momentum in this hour. The purpose of this agenda is to sway the church toward a radical political movement and the spread of socialism in our nation.

Its socialist agenda consists of some of the following buzz words:

Social justice

Environment

Racism

White privilege

Feeding the poor

The Left has a deceptive way of saying things. It's called euphemism. They call abortion "women's reproductive health care". They call gun confiscation "gun safety"; they call gay marriage "love"; they call high taxes "fair share"; they call communism "common good", and socialism "equality." They call Islamic invasion of the West "immigration", and Islamic takeover "diversity".

They will use this terminology to persuade professing Christians into buying their bill of goods. Young people especially are being hoodwinked by these socialists. They will mention these buzzwords without ever mentioning moral biblical issues. Their language is always very nuanced and overt. They use leftist talking points dressed in Christian veneer. Why have they gone after the Church?

Because the Church is the last bulwark preventing their socialist ideology from becoming a reality. But they are infiltrating the Church in subtle ways. They operate through the peace movement, the black-lives-matter movement, the women's movement, and the labor movement. They infiltrate our sacred institutions that people have considered safe. There are many examples of this.

For instance, World Vision, a once-trusted Christian adopting agency for children, has been co-opted into the leftist movement. The progressive left used to hate World Vision because of its Christian, conservative stance and charity. Now they love the organization and are becoming partners with it.

The NAE (National Association of Evangelicals) is another example. This organization was led by a full-fledged apostate, who was funded by George Soros, as are many of these secret socialists.

The Roman Catholic Church is the longest-standing example of being connected to the socialist/communist movement. And if you'll do your research, you'll find that the current Pope Francis (real name is Jorge Mario Bergoglio from Argentina) is himself a communist.

Along with the Roman Catholic Church, the mainstream Lutheran Church and Episcopalian Church have been infiltrated by socialist/communistic ideology since the 1920s and 1930s. It's been subtle, but you can see the erosion of pure doctrine in these churches, which is a direct result of the penetration of a global socialist agenda.

What is presently shocking and very disturbing is the heavy penetration of socialism into the evangelical churches over the last few years, including — get this — the Baptist Church. Find that hard to believe?

Socialism has been hidden for decades in our nation but has secretly and quietly advanced until now, when many people, including Christians, are being seduced by it. There are now elected congressmen in our government who were taught socialism at a young age in schools and universities both here and abroad. These are the progressives who seek to destroy America's ideals, form of democracy, and way of life. They have dressed up their agenda with Christian rhetoric for many years, but now they are brasher and bolder than they've ever been. Trump's presidency is the biggest reason. He is a huge threat to their plans for a socialist nation.

AMERICA'S GREATNESS: RENEWED DESTINY OR DESTRUCTION?

George Soros is a multi-billionaire hard core socialist who has had connections with Russia and Hungary for many decades, since World War II. In recent times, he has contributed more than $18 billion into the socialist/communist movement in America. His motivation is to bring down our democratic system and godly constitution by flooding the church with socialist propaganda. For example, he and his minions use amnesty for illegal immigrants as a hot button issue to bring division in our nation. Soros is a globalist and wants a borderless socialist world where America is just one small province of a greater United Nations world super state. This man's evil agenda needs to be fully exposed and resisted.

Of course, any serious Christian would say that they want nothing to do with Soros, but what they don't understand is that he uses people that we know and trust to subvert and co-opt us into his socialist agenda and movement. For this reason, many of our largest Christian institutions have been infiltrated with leftist propaganda.

As another example, Tim Keller, who formed the Gospel Coalition, has been co-opted by the left to alter doctrine and create new voters for the left. A majority of black Americans, as well as a good number of Hispanics and whites, have swallowed their agenda hook, line, and sinker.

When socialism/communism began to infiltrate churches, they preached their ideology with a little Christian veneer, and many saw through their agenda and left. But now they preach 80-90 percent Christianity and add a little of the other. They push for social justice, promote the war against global warming, the ending of white privilege, the push for illegal immigration and catering to refugees from overseas. **What many Christians don't realize is that these programs are all left-wing socialist/communist programs. You are getting 80-90 percent Christian content with a little poisonous socialist/communist doctrine thrown in.**

Please understand that the most effective lie is the one with the most truth in it. There's an old Arab proverb that says, *"Every liar tells the truth."*

There was a famous Marxist school that was established in America in the 1930s by communist Marxist refugees. It was these refugees who started the cultural and sexual revolution of the 1960s and '70s. What is happening now is that their movement has grown, and their ideology has spread to universities and now to the churches.

Christians need great discernment in this day and hour. Many are falling for these Marxist programs that have nothing to do with the gospel and they are subtly being moved to the left. These voters will end up destroying the America we've always known and loved unless the Church wakes up and rises up to an uncompromisingly righteous position of strength. Christians who actually apply their faith to politics are the great final barrier to this corrupt socialist/communist agenda. This is why they are now being targeted.

These revelations and findings are going to shock the Church and the world. I believe it could spark the radical, moral, and cultural revolution we so desperately need in our day.

WE NEED TO BE ENLIGHTENED TO THE LEFTIST ANTICHRIST AGENDA

True Christians don't really fit into America's two-party system because it's too uneven. But we must do all we can to stand for truth, righteousness, and justice in this very evil day, when all that is pure and decent is under assault. We must be enlightened to the extremely overt efforts to infiltrate and advance the liberal leftist anti-Christ agenda.

The reason their agenda seems to be advancing is because it is happening in what most people consider safe environments and institutions. Their talking points are deceptive because they are dressed with Christian veneer. They are hijacking every aspect of our culture and pushing it toward socialism, but that has never been God's divine design and purpose for America.

The Left operates through the "peace" movement, the "black lives matter" movement, the women's movement, the labor movement, etc., and they've infiltrated the Church by dressing it up with Christian rhetoric for many years. I heard from a reliable source and also read that the communist-socialist agenda has been infiltrating the Roman Catholic church and the mainstream Lutheran and Episcopalian churches since the 1920s and '30s. Do your own search. But what is most shocking and disturbing is the heavy penetration into the evangelical churches over the last few years, including southern Baptists, and as I stated, organizations like World Vision. Yes, they've been co-opted by the leftist movement. As I stated, the left-wing Maoist press used to hate World Vision with a passion because of their highly conservative stance and evangelical Christian charity, but now they love them and are partnering with them.

Furthermore, within the Gospel Coalition and Southern Baptist Convention, there have been many findings of George Soros direct-linked funds and ties to people within these organizations. I know it's hard for some to believe. As another example, Jim Wallis is one who is tied to him and has attempted to make homosexuality more acceptable and mainstream—all funded by Soros, an atheist. He is a complete evil menace to true Christianity, and churches should have nothing to do with him.

Of course, true Christians would say that they want nothing to do with Soros, but again, what they don't understand is that the method Soros and his minions use is to utilize people that the Christian community knows, respects, and trusts. Name recognition is a large part of their deception to subvert and co-opt people of faith.

Some professing Christians are interested in global warming, ending white privilege, supporting Black Lives Matter, etc., but what they fail to realize is that these are all Marxist-type programs and word-

41

construct that have nothing to do with the gospel or the kingdom of God. This is how they are gradually moving these Christians and American voters to the Left, which will end up destroying this country as we know it unless this process is reversed. Christians who apply their faith to their politics are the great barrier to the Left, but that seems to be changing as they are now the target.

The aforementioned names like Tim Keller, Jim Wallis, and others like Russell Moore and those associated with the Gospel Coalition are injecting 95% truth, but it's the 5% rat poison that is slowly diminishing truth and power in the Church. However, their pace has quickened since President Trump's election, and it's easy to see how they've ramped up and doubled down on their efforts. They've gotten more brazen, too, and are getting away with much more, like telling Christians not to be political and that they don't need to be in a two-party system. The more righteous votes they can take away from the people, the better it will serve their global socialist agenda.

At the same time, some of these socialist adherents bash conservative Christians in national newspapers like the *New York Times* and *Washington Post*. It's a left-wing movement that bashes true conservatives, glorifies their own liberal agenda, while encouraging Christians to remain neutral. At this point, however, neutrality is sinful and a traitor to the highest cause of the gospel and the saving of the God-given sovereignty and purpose of our nation.

Dr. Russell Moore leads The Southern Baptist ERLC (Evangelical Religious Liberty Commission) that used to be much more conservative and reliable, too, but not any more. For example, they conducted a meeting right before mid-term elections on how to combat conservatism. People that are connected to Moore have written many anti-conservative articles and have made it cool and hip to be an anti-Christian conservative. Young pastors are coming out of seminary thinking it's cool to hate America and bash on conservatism. Hundreds of them listen to people like Moore and think he's great, but the truth is that Moore was actually once a staffer for a Democratic congressman.

The point of this discussion is not to champion the Republican party for there are many RINOS (Republicans in name only) now in office who are not true conservatives nor Christians. It's not a matter of party, but of principle, truth, and righteous values. Christians must be enlightened as to the subversive un-Christian teaching that is going on to co-opt people into voting for a hidden liberal, global, and socialist agenda or remaining neutral. That is the crime and one of the reasons for this book.

The Left are quite adept at co-opting and twisting language and terminology to make them mean something different. One of the things they are trying to do now is redefine what "pro-life" is. They're now saying that it doesn't mean you oppose abortion or the protection of the unborn, but that it is now equivalent to taking care of the poor. I kid you not. I had a discussion recently on Facebook with a young naive Christian woman who was saying the same thing.

To be "pro-life" now also means to care about climate change and the world we live in—to be concerned about the environment and so forth. This line of thinking is spreading, and its one of the ways the Christian base is being neutralized. Homosexuality is also being redefined now as same-sex-attracted Christians and not LGBT. This is another one of the liberal-left efforts to ramp up acceptance of homosexuality in churches.

There's a religious coup going on in the Southern Baptist ERLC. As I stated, they used to be one of the most conservative organizations but are being co-opted by the Left and swinging that way.

It's not just the liberals who are doing this but others who are connected to hard core Marxists/communists like Jim Wallis. You can trace these operations back to the Communist Party USA, and the Democratic Socialists of America, who have people planted in high positions all throughout many theological seminaries. There are also several black pastors who are members of the religious commission of the Communist Party USA. There are others who are members of the National Council of Churches, and the Russian Orthodox Church, which by the way, is a tool of the KGB.

I know that for many this might be difficult to believe — and it runs pretty sinister and deep — but this is an organized Marxist program to pervert and corrupt American Christianity and to take this nation down from the inside. Wolves have infiltrated Christianity and are baiting and alluring God's people away from the truth of the gospel in order to destroy them. Preachers are not only to preach the real gospel but to courageously and aggressively defend it. And the only way to really do that is by exposing the lies and deception of the liberal-leftist, global, and socialist agenda.

*** *Most of the information in this chapter is taken from the documentary movie, Enemies Within the Church, projected to premiere sometime in 2020. Please support it, and go see it.*

CHAPTER 6

AMERICA IS NOW A HOMOSEXUAL NATION

I had one Christian woman reprove me for making such a statement about America. She said, "I am taking a moment now so that you might take a step back and consider the headline you posted about our nation. Is that what you really believe? Is that your statement of faith before the Lord about the nation?"

Due to her taking offense, this woman misunderstood the entire point of this chapter and unfollowed me.

Don't let the title of this chapter throw you, but hear me out. Yes, America is now known as a homosexual nation. By that I mean it is run and dominated by a homosexual agenda and now even a transgender agenda. And yet homosexuals are only 3-4% of our population. They control the cultural conversation, our media, our educational system, and language. You can no longer counsel gays or transgenders without backlash and persecution. You can no longer talk about family values because it offends them.

The homosexual agenda controls our movies and television. Recently a headline read that they are demanding that 20% of television characters be gay by 2025. Homosexuals control aspects of our government and our laws. Never did I think this could ever happen in America. Our forefathers are rolling over in their graves.

But guess what? Of course, the majority of our nation are not homosexuals. It's just that the 3-4% have been resolute and demonstrated resolve and dominated the majority, who are indifferent. They lie better than the Church tells the truth. The radicality that the Church should have been demonstrating for righteousness, the homosexuals have demonstrated for evil. Shame on us.

History teaches us that in the American Revolution, only about one-third of the people in the young colonies were truly patriots seeking independence from Britain's tyrannical government. Another third were loyalists to the king, while the remaining 33-40% were indifferent and didn't care one way or the other. That is how it is today.

Those old patriots had a depth of conviction and were unflinching in their resolve. They were committed to their freedom and liberty. "Give me liberty or give me death" was their desperate battle cry. They had great courage for a cause that would extend to their children, grandchildren, and future generations. Sacrifice and suffering were embraced as virtues. They defined their moment. It's time for some real spiritual patriots to arise who won't give up until there's reformation and revival in our land and in the world.

God needs only a small, consecrated company. It's actually a consistent theme in the Scriptures that a minority is what He prefers. Gideon's 300 were enough, and they recaptured seven years of a lost harvest from thousands of the enemies of God (Judges 7). The 120 in the upper room were enough (Acts 2). They were a threat to the Roman Empire who shook their world and turned it upside down for Christ. God has a mighty remnant who have not bowed their knee to Baal, and they can change this nation and the world.

As I heard someone say recently, we are in a defining moment in history, when what is done in that moment will affect the future. A defining moment is a moment that puts a nation, a culture, and a Church on a different path. A defining moment is a moment when conformity to society and the status quo is challenged. It's a pushback moment when the church rises up in defiance against the rule and political correctness of the culture. A defining moment boldly proclaims to Satanic forces, *"Who is this uncircumcised Philistine that he should defy the armies of the living God?"* (1 Sam. 17:26b).

Someone once said: Fear and anxiety typically corral us into formatted behavior, as Israel and young David's brothers displayed toward Goliath, rather than insight and revelation, which David possessed and which offers a better way. God's way is a better way.

Defining moments are those when someone takes the pen, and with decisive authorship, writes the script for a new play. It's time to write a different ending to the play the world has written, and it's time to write it in accordance with God's Word.

We are moving into a defining and tipping-point moment. Defining moments are not defined by governments or politicians. They are defined by a righteous radical remnant who refuse to let anti-Christ people with corrupt agendas define the moment. God gives us courage and authority to define moments. He expects us to be good soldiers. Throughout history, it's been the radicals in the Church who define pivotal times and crisis in culture.

Karl Marx was wrong about many things, but he was right about this: The 2-3% percent who are passionate dominate the 97-98% who are indifferent. Indifference and passivity always lose. We need to end the delusional thinking that it takes the majority to bring forth radical change. If God be for us, the odds will always be in our favor.

"What then shall we say to these things? If God is for us, who can be against us?" (Rom. 8:31).

In the kingdom of God, numbers never determine victories. God and His heavenly host are for radical righteousness. Heaven's cloud of witnesses are cheering us on in this final hour. All we need is a resolute minority anointed by the Spirit with some iron resolve to accomplish God's purposes and change history.

May You, oh Lord, infuse iron resolve into our souls for Your great glory. In Jesus' name. Amen.

CHAPTER 7

THREE PORTALS OF DEMONIC ENTRY DESTROYING AMERICA

"For our fight is not against flesh and blood, but against principalities, against powers, against the rulers of the darkness of this world, and against spiritual forces of evil in the heavenly places" (Eph. 6:12).

"It is the duty of the clergy to accommodate their discourses to the times, to preach against such sins as are most prevalent, and recommend such virtues as are most wanted." — President John Adams

Those who are familiar with my writings know I don't usually mince words. The devil is always behind sugar-coated truth and a slimy tongue. Be sure of that.

Abortion, homosexuality, and Islam are some of the greatest dangers facing America in the 21st century. Each of them has opened up portals of entry into our culture and way of life. These are ideologies that have infiltrated the minds of multitudes—shaped and fueled by the unprincipled, mad media. Much of the media carries and transmits the anti-Christ spirit.

ABORTION

I'll keep my comments brief here as I've devoted the entirety of Chapter 10 to this national sin.

Abortion is not an opinion about what women have a right to do or not do with their bodies. That's the devil's facade to hide what it really is. Willful abortion is murder at any point of a woman's pregnancy. It's a demon just like the Old Testament god of Molech, to whom people sacrificed babies. It's the same altar where many Americans now worship.

Think about it. Why are there abortion rights that have killed 60 million babies in America alone? Straight answer: mainly because of fornication and adultery.

There are some cases of rape and so forth, but that's a very small minority. Yet it's one of the main talking points of what people debate on. It's hogwash. Sexual immorality is the biggest reason we have abortions. Schools are indoctrinating children in sex education to expand the abortion industry. People want sex without the commitment and covenant of marriage and responsibility of the consequences. In fact, what they say with their actions is "A baby will ruin my happiness, so kill it!" How much more self-centered and demonic can it be?

But do you know what is fueling the increase of promiscuous sex and now pedophilia, as well as all sorts of perversion? One word: Pornography. If you shut down the billion-dollar pornography industry, you will radically decrease sexual immorality and perversion on every level. Abortions will also decrease exponentially.

Pornography is another portal of entry for demonic access. These evils are all linked together. It's Satan's master plan and worldwide web.

But honestly, decreasing abortions should not be the goal. The goal is to completely outlaw it and legislate against it.

HOMOSEXUALITY

How about homosexuality? I wrote an article more than four years ago on homosexuality being a demon, and demons flew from every direction to attack my words. People were calling our ministry phone, writing nasty comments, sharing the article with right-wing watch groups and mocking it. They were fuming in venomous rage.

That alone proves it was a demon because it's the very point that nearly everyone attacked.

People accused me of having no compassion, but guess what? I also received calls and messages from homosexuals who knew I was telling the truth and wanted help. My compassion was directed toward those.

Now, it's not only acceptable in our culture, but it's celebrated and legalized. What happened? Demons, through the agency of deceived people and God-hating lawmakers, pushed it through and legalized it. When they did, it opened up a larger portal of entry for the release of more demons and the rule of a principality in our nation.

As long as the majority of people want their demons, God will let them have them, because He honors the human agency of free will—a debased mind, devoid of judgment, will be their most terrible portion (Rom. 1:24-28). Eventually homosexuality will destroy the culture of a nation and bring down the judgment of God as it did in days of old. Wherever homosexuality is prevalent, and alas, made law, evil rules and reigns, and anyone who fights it is preyed upon.

Here is something very interesting again that I picked up in a conversation with my minister friend, John Fenn (refer to his comments on abortion in Chapter 10 from this same exchange).

Have you seen this old quote from Gore Vidal?: *"Actually, there is no such thing as a homosexual person, any more than there is such a thing as a heterosexual person. The words are adjectives describing sexual acts, not people..."* (From Gore Vidal: Sexually Speaking). The fact is that the word "homosexual" wasn't invented until 1892, when a German book on sexual perversions was translated into English (*Psychopathia Sexualis* was the German book).

God created male and female with sexual union between the two being first for procreation; anything outside that is merely behavior.

In 1 Corinthians 6:9 and 1 Timothy 1:10, some translations unfortunately use the word "homosexual," when actually there is no Greek word for that (the Bible was canonized way before 1892). The word that is used in the aforementioned references is "*arsenokoites*," and it just describes a male-to-male sexual union. Behavior. The Bible mentions no other gender besides male and female. There is no gender called "homosexual" or "transgender" either. That is a behavior.

This fact has been lost on millions of people across America and now the world. Even Christians have subtly allowed homosexual behavior to be elevated to the status of gender in their minds. The LGBTQ movement seeks to elevate their behavior to gender status. But one of their best-known members, Gore Vidal, had it right. To paraphrase again, sex is a behavior, not a gender. We see the leftists' efforts in the courts and in society to change that. It's a lie that Western culture in particular has swallowed. But the truth is, there are men, and there are women. The rest is behavior.

ISLAM

Now this one will make people even more angry. The mask to Islam is that it's a nice religion of peace. Much of the gullible populace has swallowed this lie — hook, line, and sinker.

Have you ever read the Quran and the ideologies that are written therein?

The Quran says:

- Muslims must not take infidels as friends (3:28).

- Any religion other than Islam is unacceptable (3:85).

- Maim and crucify the infidels if they criticize Islam (5:33).

- Terrorize and behead those who believe in Scriptures other than the Quran (8:12).

- Muslims must muster all weapons to terrorize the infidels (8:60).

- The unbelievers are stupid; urge the Muslims to fight them (8:65).

- When opportunity arises, kill the infidels wherever you catch them (9:5).

- The Jews and the Christians are perverts; fight them (9:29).

- Make war on the infidels living in your neighborhood (9:23).

According to its own "holy" (really, unholy) book, this is a religion full of hate that believes it does God a service by killing all non-Muslims, especially Christians and Jews. Jesus warned us of such.

"They will put you out of the synagogues. Yes, the time is coming that whoever kills you will think that he is offering a service to God" (John 16:2).

Yes, some Muslims are good, peaceful Americans, but when push comes to shove, most of them will stand with their ideology. Concerning President Trump's stopping Muslim immigration, consider the following:

With regard to Muslim immigration to this country, why do we not consider the underlying belief system, Islam, upon which the Muslim religion is founded? Consider some of Islam's teachings:

1. There are only two classes of people in the world, Muslims and infidels.

2. Infidels are to be assimilated, even if by force, into the Muslim religion.

3. Infidels who refuse to be assimilated are to be killed.

4. Child marriage. One of Muhammad's wives was six years old.

5. It is a husband's privilege to beat a disobedient wife.

6. No Muslim wife has the right to divorce her husband.

Above all, Muslims, in their quest for world domination are granted permission to pretend they are abandoning certain tenets of their faith to obtain a foothold in countries they intend to assimilate into Islam. The name of this doctrine is *taqiyya*. Originally it was a Shia Muslim-only practice, but the Sunnis now practice it for the same purpose. It has been used throughout the ages to make Muslims more palatable to Christians and other faiths. Muslims are encouraged to take over communities by sheer force of numbers. Once having gotten a numerical advantage, hidden Islamic beliefs begin to surface. Dearborn, Michigan is an example. The Mayor, the police chief, and a majority of the city council are Muslims. Not long ago sharia law began to be practiced there. When federal authorities stepped in and declared sharia law illegal, they simply changed the name of the sharia courts to "Family Counseling Centers," where they still practice sharia law.

The bottom line is this: In light of *taqiyya* how can we ever trust Muslims to be what they present themselves to be? Muslims in France have now dropped all pretenses of being anything else than fully practicing their faith — with the exception of killing the infidel. One can only wonder how long that will last. No one can now be elected President without the Muslim vote. This is in and of itself a danger that keeps unlawful Muslim practices spreading.

Because of this practice of *taqiyya,* no one ever knows for sure what the Muslim next door really believes. We are inundated constantly with "radical Muslims" being responsible for atrocities. Could it be they are not radical at all but rather simply devout Muslims practicing their faith to the fullest?

The more people understand the entire Islamic strategy to kill and conquer, the more society will wake up to it, and the better it will be for America and its future. This religious war is filled with deliberately thought-out, methodical strategies to take over every nation Islam enters. It's called *jihad.* This dark Islamic strategy is so much bigger than the average person realizes. The big plan jihadists have devised for America is to destroy it from within.

Take note of the similarities between abortion, homosexuality, and Islam. Abortion is death to the most innocent. Homosexuality is death to the family, normal reproduction, and the increase of confusion and perversion. Transgenderism came in right behind homosexuality to pile on more confusion, darkness, and death upon the human race. Finally, Islam declares death to all nations who do not worship their false god.

Death has gained great access into America. We are in a very serious and intense war, but many Americans are still oblivious to it. Satan is playing for keeps. It is time for every believer in Jesus Christ to enter this spiritual fight and stop living in denial. It's time for fire to erupt in the bellies of preachers and for their mouths to thunder truth and righteousness. Quit being passive and politically correct. In doing so, you are actually being an ally to the evil. It's time to rock the boat and demolish the strongholds in people's minds through not only heartfelt, fervent prayer, but through strong, straightforward preaching.

"For the weapons of our warfare are not carnal, but mighty through God to the pulling down of strongholds, casting down imaginations and every high thing that exalts itself against the knowledge of God, bringing every thought into captivity to the obedience of Christ" (2 Cor. 10:4-5).

CHAPTER 8

THE LEFTIST NARRATIVE: DIVORCE CHRISTIANITY FROM THE BIBLE

Secularized America is steeped deeply in gross darkness. Our youth are Satan's prized trophy. Without effectual, fervent intercession and a compassionate, convicting message confirmed with miracles, most don't stand a chance to ever experience true conversion and receive the life of God.

The lies of the fake media are shaping the minds of Americans, especially our youth. They've been lied to about their identity and who they are. They've been lied to about history, politics, racism, and socialism. They've been lied to about creation, God, and religion — brainwashed into seeing Christianity and Judaism in a bad light while being taught that Islam and other Eastern religions are good.

I have friends who work in the secular field, and they tell me that more and more young people they work with have completely lost their identity and are yielding to homosexuality, lesbianism, and transgenderism. One friend of mine told me that every other student in his drivers-education class is a transgender.

AMERICA IS SICKER THAN YOU THINK

This unclean spirit has disconnected many of our youth (although it has affected all ages) from their natural instincts and connected them to confusion, as they cling to another of like gender, hoping to fill the gaping hole of emptiness in their hearts. Tampering with your DNA and who your Creator made you is simply spiritual rebellion that stems from entertaining these unclean spirits, which the lies and ideologies in our culture have unleashed.

They can talk about the abuse they've experienced or the pain, the neglect, and the emptiness they feel, and sincere believers can't help but be moved with compassion. But we didn't have this sort of confusion and highly visible perversion a generation ago. In fact, we'd have been appalled back then if we could have foreseen what would be so prevalent in America today. Do we even understand that all these things signify one of the last stages of the death of a culture? Read Romans 1.

People might say that homosexuality has been around for thousands of years, but what about gay marriage and transgenderism?

This is a part of a much larger picture and grand Satanic strategy to continue to infect and further break down the moral base of our society, harass and weaken the Church, and separate more of America from the moral absolutes of the Bible and what this nation was founded upon. Our first president, George Washington, said that the issues of virtue and morality are indispensable.

Satan is no longer hiding his cards.

In case you haven't noticed, this is America today: Drag queens in our schools. Pedophiles in our Boys Scouts. Increased and intensified discrimination against true Christianity. Students can wear satanic T-shirts to school but cannot pray in the name of Jesus. Teachers won't read or discuss the Scriptures with students for fear of parental prosecution. Counseling transgenders or gays is forbidden. Teenagers can get abortions on demand without parental permission. In my area, witches are cursing churches and now incanting the queer spirit over our region, while many lukewarm Christians sleep and slumber through it all. Too many still think this is a game, and the greatest danger is that we don't see the danger.

Things that were shameful and kept hidden not too long ago are now flaunted and paraded in the open. If not for a holy, praying remnant who serve as the final firewall and salt and light in our nation, it would be hopeless. Neither Republicans nor Democrats nor Independents nor socialists nor communists can deliver the soul of this nation.

Satan is the god of this world (2 Cor. 4:4), and the prince of the power of the air (Eph. 2:2), and he specializes in blinding the minds of those who are perishing.

"But even if our gospel is veiled, it is veiled to those who are perishing, whose minds the god of this age has blinded, who do not believe, lest the light of the gospel of the glory of Christ, who is the image of God, should shine on them."

Still, too many believers have become desensitized and dulled to the madness of this anti-Christ spirit, and too many pastors and church leaders remain silent or have yielded to gross compromise. The battle for believers is now for a unified kingdom and a remnant Church that will stand as one.

TWO SIDES

There are two sides to this matter. One side is exemplified by the remarks made sometime ago by the gay mayor from Indiana named Pete Buttigieg, who, by the way, proclaims unashamedly that his Creator made him gay, and if anyone has an issue with that, they should take it up with Him. And he even offered to have a national discussion on what is a scriptural Christian. We should take him up on that one, although it might be a trap.

The liberal left is now making this a religious thing. It's a new attack. Just watch. The plan going forward is to divorce Christianity from the Bible. They won't tell you that now, but that is their strategy, especially as we get closer to the next election.

The leftists are desperate and in a frenzy, because they can't stand the thought of President Trump being elected for another four years. Look for another false narrative they'll serve up to the American people about Trump's connection to Bible-believing Christians. Their true colors are now being seen by many Americans, and their strategy will backfire and fail.

Here's the other side to this matter: If you stand up to the LGBTQ agenda, society will ask for your head a la John the Baptist. The most recent case in point is the young Australian rugby player who was fired for essentially quoting Galatians 5:19-21, and saying that sinners, including homosexuals, are headed to hell if they don't repent. To add insult to the injury of being fired, instead of defending him, the most visible charismatic leader in Australia published an article condemning the brother for being unloving. This is so typical of our day, and one of the reasons the church has little power and authority. How can the church stand when we are so divided on the most basic Scriptural issues of sin and repentance?

TIME FOR HOLY ZEAL

Shouldn't we all be rallying behind our fearless brother in support of his statements? Shouldn't we applaud him for boldly voicing his faith? Shouldn't we proclaim with him the Word of God and tell the world that our God, who made us male and female, is deserving of all our loyalty and worship? Instead, too many professing Christians, even in so-called Pentecostal/Charismatic camps, promote a false Christ and persecute those who proclaim the one, true God.

This is the anti-Christ spirit that separates Christianity from the Bible and has opened the door to seducing spirits, who are deceiving multitudes.

All professing Christians need to wake up and come out from this Babylonian system, and stand in solidarity when such condemnation is heaped on our brothers and sisters who are standing for truth, morality, and righteousness. The world expresses outrage at our stand for righteousness, and many in the Church agree with the world and find fault with the righteous; they accuse them of being unloving, condemning, and even homophobic. This should not be. Our brother may have been a little overzealous in his approach, but so what? It doesn't mean we take the opposing view and condemn him for it.

Where is the honor and the zeal for God's house and God's holiness? Where are those who are jealous for God's name? Where is the spirit of the early apostles, who, in the midst of intense persecution, proclaimed, *"It is better to obey God than man?"*

CHAPTER 9

IT'S TIME TO END THE LIBERAL LEFTIST MOVEMENT

The leftists hate our Independence Day/July 4th celebrations. This past year Facebook and Google, owned by leftist-liberals censored some pictures of American flags and portraits of American heroes and fallen soldiers on both Memorial Day and Independence Day. Some Democratic presidential candidates put the darkest spin possible on these national holidays. They even display anger toward President Trump for wanting to celebrate the 4th of July. My brain freezes on that one.

The writing is on the wall. We have a brief window of opportunity to buy up more time for a national miracle and the restoration of America's destiny. This is not overreach or a hyper-dramatic statement. It is reality.

The leftists heap disdain on the sacrifice of heroes. They rail against every iota of American patriotism. Most of all, they lie about our history, our Founding Fathers, and they deny the role of Christianity in the founding of our nation. They've reached the point of desperation and will do anything for votes in 2020.

For example, at this writing, we are witnessing a human tragedy at our southern border. Dr. James Dobson made a trip down there and said this about it:

"This is all happening because politicians have created a system that turns these migrants into political pawns. This is the system set up by a liberal congress and judges. It is a well-known fact that President Obama's administration established many of these unworkable

policies, and congress is steadfastly unwilling to change them. *Every effort at reform has been overridden or ignored. It is set in stone. Democrats want massive numbers of immigrants who will someday become voters. Some Republicans support the policies because they want cheap labor for agricultural purposes. The border could be fixed, but there are very few in authority who seem to care.*" (article, *Dr. Dobson Tours Border, June 2019*)

South Africa is further down the road, and we could learn so much from such nations. Here is a recent comment on Facebook from one of its residents soliciting our prayers:

"*I live in Johannesburg, South Africa, and every day it's such a struggle for our nation. We are living with some of the lowest education levels in the world. Our universities have always been world-class, but standards have dropped. For 60 years, during Apartheid, black folks weren't allowed to pass the same exams as whites (we are now experiencing the fallout from this).*

"*There are 3 million white folks and 60 million blacks left in South Africa. In the nearly three decades since Apartheid ended our country has made little progress. God has been taken out of our education system, too.*

"*Please pray for our education system and all our higher education facilities. We have extreme greed, and nepotism, and our municipalities have been used as banks because folks who can afford to pay for municipal services don't. We have open borders to neighboring countries who are worse off than we are, so they all come here. Our electricity department was looted by the people from our previous government, and our South African airline is broke. We need prayers.*"

I don't mean to be callous, but the idiocy of South Africa's citizens have brought these conditions forward. The wool was pulled over their eyes, and now the nation suffers.

In political jargon, *"useful idiot"* is a term for people perceived as propagandists for a cause whose goals they are not fully aware of, and who are used cynically by the leaders of the cause.

As I stated earlier, in many ways, present-day America reminds me of the sinking of the *Titanic*, when musicians played their final song before succumbing to their death. We've had so many opportunities to right the ship, but we keep drinking the vile Kool-Aid that our wicked politicians and corrupt media are serving us while puncturing the ship with more holes. Indeed, we've become a ship of fools. We've had plenty of reasons to do something different, but instead, we've defiantly said "No" to righteousness at nearly every turn. Groaning and mourning always increases under the rule of wicked politicians.

"When the righteous are in authority, the people rejoice; but when the wicked rule, the people mourn" (Prov. 29:2).

THE CYCLE OF BONDAGE

In 1887 Alexander Tyler, a Scottish history professor at the University of Edinburgh, had this to say about the fall of the Athenian Republic some 2,000 years prior:

"A democracy is always temporary in nature; it simply cannot exist as a permanent form of government.

"A democracy will continue to exist up until the time that voters discover that they can vote themselves generous gifts from the public treasury.

"From that moment on, the majority always votes for the candidates who promise the most benefits from the public treasury, with the result that every democracy will finally collapse over loose fiscal policy, which is always followed by a dictatorship.

"The average age of the world's greatest civilizations from the beginning of history, has been about 200 years.

"During those 200 years, these nations always progressed through the following sequence:

"From bondage to spiritual faith;

From spiritual faith to great courage;

From courage to liberty;

From liberty to abundance;

From abundance to complacency;

From complacency to apathy;

From apathy to dependence;

From dependence back into bondage."

President Trump is not our savior, but his election victory in 2016 tells me that the people of this country have had enough of the establishment. They are waking up to the global liberal agenda, and many don't want it. For clear evidence, look at the large turnouts and great excitement at Trump's rallies.

AMERICA AT A CROSSROADS

In 2008 and 2012, millions of professing Christians either voted for Obama or did not vote at all. Professing Christians who voted for such a wicked and evil man still need to repent, because it was his administration that opened the door wide to such filth, evil, hatred, division and perversion that now fills our nation. You cannot call yourself a Christian while promoting evil.

- You can't vote that way anymore without being an ally to Satan and evil.

- You can no longer wink at sin and endorse wicked politicians.

- You can't remain silent while full-term baby killing is now made legal.

- You can't stick your nose up at God, whom the Democratic National Committee has rejected.

- You can't continue to endorse darkness, death, and destruction — open borders, sanctuary cities, full-term abortion, anti-Israel agendas, same-sex marriage, globalism, and socialism.

Stop sowing to the wind if you want to stop reaping the whirlwind.

If you endorse these things ignorantly, the mercy of God is still available to you, but if you support these things willingly, you're under the judgment of God.

LACK OF CHARACTER AND DISCERNMENT IS THE ISSUE

The problem is that a large segment of professing American Christians lack character and discernment, and they endorse the same.

John Wooden observed, "*Your character is what you really are. Your reputation is only what others think you are.*" Poor discernment and the failure to see things as they really are is colored by the condition of one's heart.

Many have a reputation of being someone great in public, but who they are at home is who they really are. Many need to repent because their walk does not match their talk. Hypocrisy is the Church's subtle leaven.

So many of those who profess Jesus Christ continually vote for the Democratic Party. How can you justify that when they are now riding fully with Satan? Today, I dare call them "the Demonic Party."

Stop voting for criminals to fill governmental positions in our land. How can so many have such a high tolerance for the corruption and tyranny they represent? It's pure madness and defies logic.

Godless Hollywood and the snake-oiled media will keep endorsing evil. It's about time you stop believing their lies.

Why do you even give the time of day to Trump-haters and networks like CNN, who lie continually and poison you with fake news?

THE ROOT IS HYPOCRISY

Again, the problem is in the Church world. We have too many hypocrites who tell us they love Jesus out of one side of their mouth while casting votes for those who represent the devil's agenda. Please educate yourselves with Biblical values.

When you vote for any politician, be it senator, governor, mayor, or representative who is a baby-killer, a God-hater, an enemy of Israel, and pervert-promoter — among many other evils — you are one giant-sized hypocrite. You are serving the devil's agenda, not the living God.

When you're ruled by materialism, you don't have a moral compass. When you believe the lying media, your judgment is blinded. When you're a slave to man, God is not your master. When you don't fear God, you have no discernment. It then becomes impossible to differentiate between the holy and the profane, the clean and the unclean, and the good and the evil.

This is the problem in America. Elections mirror who we are as a nation and identify the lack of a true moral base in our culture and in a large majority of the professing church. If every professing Christian voted for Biblical values, each election would produce more godly leadership at every level.

When you, as a professing Christian, are swimming with the tide of pop culture and following the most popular TV preachers, who cannot call homosexuality a sin, who cannot speak of the cross and the blood, who will never say the word "repent," who endorsed Barack Obama and Hillary Clinton for president, who are motivated by publicity, popularity, and earthly gain, you are in the devil's grip.

Please hear me on this. Obama is like a modern-day Nebuchadnezzar whom God used to bring judgment to America. The divine purpose was to separate those who truly love Christ from those who don't and to shake everything that can be shaken. The present division in our nation is simply the revealing of people's hearts — that now those who put their trust in God, as opposed to those who put their trust in man may be revealed. From here and moving forward, our nation will never be the same, but this division between light and darkness will continue to widen. The revealing and manifestation of this spiritual war and division has begun.

The following scripture is so compelling for the time we are in.

"Many shall be purified, and made white, and tried; but the wicked shall do wickedly: and none of the wicked shall understand; but the wise shall understand" (Dan. 12:10).

The wise understand what is going on, but the wicked are blinded and cannot see and understand.

Electing wicked and evil politicians for president is nearly equivalent to absolving Satan from his sins and letting him into the White House. I almost said, "letting him into heaven," but God will never allow Satan or those who follow him into heaven. Never. You must be born again and prove your repentance by your works.

That eliminates every hyper-grace, no-repentance preacher and those who've been grossly deceived by their twisted message of grace that has been turned into lasciviousness. Woe unto you, for in a time when we need the greatest repentance in our nation, you preach that no repentance is necessary and that Jesus has forgiven you of all past, present, and future sins. Your doctrine of grace is a disgrace. Please repent and come into right standing with God before it is too late.

APPEALING TO LOGIC

Think of the kind of people who hate President Trump. They are the Islamists, the communists, the socialists, the LGBTQ mafia, the Islamic regime in Iran, the Christian hating media, the drug dealers, the abortion industry, Planned Parenthood, the do-nothing Democrats, the coyotes, the globalists, Hollywood, the climate-change so-called "scientists," the deep state, and corrupt politicians. Doesn't that speak volumes?

Think of what kind of people love President Trump. The persecuted Christians around the world, Israel, the oppressed Iranian people, hard-working Americans, law-abiding people, traditional-family people, Cuban descendants, and Venezuelan descendants. Actually, I include on this list anyone with a little common sense. This alone is a good sign that he is on the right side of history and doing something good.

And so, this brings me to a conclusive question: how many of you African-American professing Christians are going to keep your Democratic Party affiliation in spite of the pure evil in it? Will you now repent and switch your allegiance? Or will you keep voting for your favorite party and your darling baby-killers?

How can you commit such a blasphemous act and vote for the killers of your own race? Unborn black children are being aborted more than any other race, and you vote for it, while at the same time saying, "Black lives matter." You are the epitome of hypocrisy.

If you are black, why did you vote for Hillary in the last election, when she admires Margaret Sanger and defends Planned Parenthood, who want to abort as many black babies as possible? Do you realize that most of those abortion clinics are in black neighborhoods?

If you are a professing Christian, why do you keep endorsing wicked men who are full of greed, have no love for the truth, and no fear of God (Ex. 18:21)? This includes Republican candidates as well.

Set aside Christian conscience for a moment, and let's just use a little logic.

- If you are a veteran, in the military, or closely related to a military member, why are you voting for a party whose secretary of state left those men to die in Benghazi and had the nerve to lie about it over and over again? They called for help, but the help was told to stand down.

- If you have a factory job, why are you endorsing a party whose members supported the Trans-Pacific Partnership? Before Trump, factory workers were being laid off because jobs were going overseas. So many unfavorable deals were made with China. Now Democrats are welcoming open borders and illegals to get benefits to be paid with your tax money.

• If you are poor, why do you endorse the Democratic Party, when most of them support Wall Street and all the big banks? Big banks keep poor people poor through destroying the poor man's credit by allowing medical bills and collections to affect your credit scores so you can pay higher interest rates than the rich — taking much of the little money you earn.

• If you carry a gun or believe in the Constitution, how can you affiliate with a party who wants to eliminate the NRA, take your guns, and abolish the Second Amendment?

• If you consider yourself a good parent, why would you vote for the Democratic Party, who promote educational programs to indoctrinate your children with sodomy and sexual perversion at such an early age?

• If you even breathe, why would you be affiliated and endorse the Democratic Party who murder the most innocent?

"America will never be destroyed from the outside. If we falter and lose our freedoms, it will be because we destroyed ourselves." — Abraham Lincoln

CIVIL WAR, LOSS OF LIBERTIES IMMINENT UNLESS THINGS CHANGE

And you who say, "God is still in control," save your speech. They said the same thing in Hitler's day when he was killing 6 million Jews. God is in control of those who have given Him control. He is in control of those who have submitted to Him. To be silent, passive, and neutral now is to be an enemy of God.

Unless a nation of useful idiots (not to be offensive, but as I already stated, in political jargon, a "useful idiot" is a derogatory term for a person perceived as a propagandist for a cause, the goals of which he or she does not fully comprehend, and who is used cynically by the leaders of the cause) wake up and come to their senses, I'm afraid we could be headed for a civil war. There are far too many unreasonable and wicked men who do not have faith within our borders and in positions of authority.

Barring supernatural intervention brought on by sincere repentance and the mercy of God, the Church may eventually have to go underground, at least in some states. California is now trying to make the Bible illegal. And some believe that, as California goes, so goes the nation. We are losing our freedoms, and as I stated, too many still think this is all a game. Persecution is intensifying right here in America.

The good news is that persecution tends to bring out the best of every church and every Christian. Persecution tends to separate the real Christian from the false, the goats from the sheep, the tares from the wheat, and the good fish from the bad fish. And that's a good thing. We don't have much persecution that is testing us yet in our nation. Most believers think it's bold and fearless just to call abortion and homosexuality a sin. Honestly, our version of Christianity is so soft.

So what can the American Church start doing now in this season of reprieve and opportunity?

Start preaching a Biblical gospel that actually delivers people from ignorance and evil, and strengthens their foundation of truth and righteousness. Stop all the self-esteem and success-in-life talks. Preach the word with the Spirit's fire.

Start getting excited about the things that excite Jesus, like the actual gospel of the kingdom and His commission to make disciples.

Stop getting excited over emotional experiences and stimuli that tickles your soul but is no threat to the kingdom of darkness.

Quit listening to celebrity preachers who tout their titles of "Apostle," "Prophet," and "Bishop," and who always seem to have a "word from God" that came from their latest conversation with an angel or a visit to heaven. Who of us is not tired of hearing the latest formula for activating blessings?

Let the uncompromisingly righteous band and bond together as never before. Be strengthened, and be emboldened. Act like it's now or never to save the *Titanic*. Brace yourselves. The Democrats will go crazy, and all hell will break loose if Trump wins a second term.

For those who are kingdom-minded and eternity-minded, our best days are still ahead. Let us seize the opportunity of a lifetime. We can save the Church and the nation. But understand that, if we finally preach the real gospel and Christians still vote for the liberal-leftist agenda, then they didn't really repent.

It is now that the nation's "useful idiots" may finally awaken when they realize that the Democratic Party and the RINOS (Republicans In Name Only) are the ones who are putting holes in the mighty *Titanic* with their attempts to sink it. And the CINOS (Christians In Name Only) must repent or else face a certain judgement.

DISCLAIMER: I am well aware that Republicans are not exempt from cooperating with the same anti-Christ agenda as the Liberal Left. There are more Republicans than ever who may still be conservative fiscally but not morally. Conservatism is nearly a farce in our nation. Both parties have moved farther and farther left in the last few decades. Our hope must no longer be in a party system. We must vote character, morality, ethics, truth, and righteous values.

CHAPTER 10

ABORTION: SATANIC PRIEST GOVERNORS FILLING UP THE CUP OF JUDGMENT

The far-left Democratic Party has become Satan's pawn. When New York Governor Andrew Cuomo signed into law full-term abortion among a gleeful group of other politicians at the beginning of 2019, Christian outrage across the nation should have gone through the roof.

Then, to add insult to injury, Virginia Governor Ralph Northam, represented his evil party well when he basically stated (paraphrased): "If a mother is in labor, the infant would be delivered and would be kept comfortable and would be resuscitated according to the mother's wishes, and then a discussion would ensue between the physicians and the mother."

I am mortified by both the wickedness of some of our politicians serving in these high positions of authority and the silence of Christ's Church and its' leaders concerning this issue. Furthermore, I was appalled by the standing ovation and loud cheers that the New York State Senate gave when they removed these abortion restrictions. Surely every Christian leader must have felt the seismic shift in their spirit as the slaughter of more innocent new borns was legislated.

What these governors did and said were the most horrifying actions and words I think I've ever heard from any politician in my lifetime. Human depravity has reached new levels as these governors proposed what amounts to a policy of infanticide. As I said, this horrific and unthinkable evil should be drawing the strong rebuke from every Christian leader and individual across America.

Outrage in the form of riots and protests should be flowing like waves across America after such blasphemous words from what has become a party of sadistic savages led by Herodian-type governors.

I do not apologize for my plain speech. To be silent now is to be allied with the murder of the most harmless, defenseless, and innocent among us. If furious and righteous indignation does not fill your soul, something is wrong with your salvation experience. Neutrality in our culture is now sinful.

If leaders, ministers, and pastors who have platforms play this down in soft-toned disingenuous speech or choose to remain silent, they are to be pitied. In the words of Martin Luther King Jr.: "*History will have to record that the greatest tragedy of this period of social transition was not the strident clamor of the bad people, but the appalling silence of the good people.*"

Decent Americans and churches of every denomination must do something now and act as a unified voice of condemnation across this land. This is the most wicked, filthy, inhumane, brutal, and barbaric act in American history, and I do not believe I'm overstating that. Do you think for a moment God Almighty will just wink at this and not demonstrate His severity on our nation?

We will see massive destruction on a scale never heretofore seen in our nation if this trend of infanticide continues and we roll our heads and turn the other way. We will see unimaginable disasters and death across our land. God will bring down what is left of the walls of protection in America.

Once again, if the aforementioned statements are too strong or a little over the top for you let me once again appeal to logic, science, and Scripture.

We find the highest purpose for sexual union between a husband and wife is procreation. Women are made by God to be able to conceive and bear children, which is why we see the submission of a mother's will to her pregnancy and the unborn baby in her womb.

As I stated earlier, in a recent interaction with a minister friend of mine, John Fenn, he made the following insightful comments concerning the abortion issue, which he gave me permission to share.

"To me, the key is our society devalued women and their ability to conceive and bear children, in the midst of women's lib. They forgot that fact, forgot that a woman can do something amazing that no man can do — conceive and nurture a human being within her body.

'All of the natural world of higher mammals shows us the amazing thing about females: They exercise free choice up to the point of conception, but once conception happens, a deeper law comes into effect that overrides and governs her free will from that point forward: Pregnancy. It is as true of the elephant and antelope as it is for human women.

"That deeper law governs how she feels, what she eats, risks she will or will not take, her sleep, her relationships — that is a deeper law proven by the fact pregnant women do alter their behavior, submitting their will to the pregnancy. That is the deeper law, the deeper principle.

"The amazing thing is a baby girl is born with all the eggs she will ever ovulate. That means there has been an unbroken chain since Eve, for today's baby girl has in her body all the eggs she will ever ovulate, as her mother had within her during her own gestation all the eggs she would ovulate. Her grandmother had her mother in her while still in her mother's womb. All the way back to the first woman (which has been proven genetically that we all came from one man and one woman).

"She has, even as a newborn, her children within her. Conversely, a man can produce 100 million sperm every half hour or so, but women are special, unique, and that has been lost in the effort to gain their rightful equality in society.

"The nurturing of a human being within her body is a deeper law. Pregnancy is the law to which a woman's free will submits. This truth is seen in mammals all over the globe — a pregnant female submits herself to the deeper (and higher) law of pregnancy. Amazing."

Now if you want to make a case against abortion using the Bible, following is a great reference to prove that God recognizes the unborn baby as life.

"If men fight, and hurt a woman with child, so that she gives birth prematurely, yet no harm follows, he shall surely be punished accordingly as the woman's husband imposes on him; and he shall pay as the judges determine. But if any harm follows, then you shall give life for life..." (Exodus 21:22-23).

In Exodus 21:22-23, the Lord gives a hypothetical situation in which two men are fighting and a pregnant woman is nearby, and in the fight she is injured and loses her baby. The Lord says if it was an accident then the woman's husband and the judges will determine a fine and punishment, but if the man's intent was assault, he must give his life for that of the baby's, life for life. This proves the point God considers the baby in the womb alive and with equal rights to those living outside the womb.

This brings up another issue worth mentioning in this book. Why are Christian leaders — and, especially, pastors of local churches — not addressing such issues?

UNMUTE THE PULPITS

New research shows that while 90 percent of pastors believe the Bible has much to say about today's pressing political and societal issues, fewer than 10 percent are talking about those issues from the pulpit.

Researcher George Barna spoke recently on American Family Radio's, "Today's Issues," about his research project over the past two years, in which the Barna Group asked pastors across the country about their beliefs regarding the relevancy of Scripture to societal, moral, and political issues, as well as the content of their sermons in light of their beliefs.

What he found was startling.

"When we asked them about all the key issues of the day, 90 percent of them are telling us, 'Yes, the Bible speaks to every one of these issues,'" Barna told American Family Radio. "Then we ask them: 'Well, are you teaching your people what the Bible says about those issues?' and the numbers drop to less than 10 percent of pastors who say they will speak to it."

Sam Rohrer, president of the American Pastors Network, says that while it is clear that there is a disconnect between knowing the truth and preaching it, the real question is "Why?" Avoiding the politically unpopular portions of Scripture is in some respects understandable from a human perspective, but from God's perspective, it is sin.

"The reality is that most people, including pastors, wish to be comfortable and to avoid controversy," Rohrer said.

"If the primary goal is to see people leave on Sunday morning feeling good about themselves and feeling comfortable rather than seeing the holiness of God and the ugly reality of sin, then a pastor will answer to God for doing his own will rather than declaring God's will. The issues of the day that confront our nation must be dealt with from the pulpit if God's Word is to make a difference in people's lives and if the culture is to be impacted. This includes the areas of marriage and divorce, life and family, pornography, abortion, homosexuality, and transgenderism, etc."

Barna added that many pastors are afraid to get involved in political issues because of the controversy it might create. And, he added:

"Controversy keeps people from being in the seats; controversy keeps people from giving money and from attending programs."

He also found that, when asked how they measure the success of their churches, most pastors look to five factors: "attendance, giving, number of programs, number of staff, and square footage."

"The fact that so many pastors are more concerned with the size of their buildings and church bank accounts than with the condition of the souls they shepherd is without excuse," Rohrer continued.

"By abdicating their responsibility as ministers of God to 'preach the Word' in favor of square footage, many pastors are, in essence, saying God's Word is not really authoritative. In reality, a pastor — or any Christian, for that matter—who feels they have the right to pick and choose what portions of Scripture they will believe or teach, rather than preach the 'whole counsel of God' have, in effect, made themselves a god."

The need to unmute American pulpits to speak the whole counsel of God has never been so vital.

Consider the recent lawless behavior of our nation and government just this year (2019):

- Remove God from everything we do and now even our swearing-in with oaths.

- Call a border wall immoral, but call killing our most innocent, "moral" and "a woman's right."

- Refuse to build a border wall or even negotiate. Instead, shut down our government and go on vacation while others suffer for your irresponsible, childish behavior.

- Scream for illegal immigration and sanctuary cities so pushers, rapists, thugs, and every kind of criminal can have refuge, but use nice, snake-oiled speech for allowing delivered babies to die on hospital tables.

- Gun down our police officers in barbaric, lawless fashion, but praise violence and out-of-control wackos.

- Take away our guns so school, street, and club shootings can stop, but don't you dare use Bibles to teach in our schools and universities.

- Enforce homosexuality, transgenderism, and every kind of perversion, but outlaw counseling that would reverse this curse and minister deliverance, sanity, and freedom to many.

- Watch Hollywood defame all that is godly and decent while labeling all who oppose them as racist, hateful, and bigoted.

- Bully those who wear MAGA hats to honor our president's vision for America and scream like a psycho lunatic — while the law does nothing about it.

- Praise the Muslims and their Islamic Baal god; praise Buddha and Eastern religions; fill our airwaves with New Age gobbledygook; praise witches, warlocks, and satanists; but mock God and His beloved Son and all that is godly, righteous, decent, and clean.

- Keep making attempts to remove every vestige of vibrant Christianity, the only hope of all mankind, from our public institutions of learning, commerce, and government.

And this is just scratching the surface.

But when murder of our most innocent after birth is made law, you have a nation on the verge of a death from which it may never recover. Our children and grandchildren will suffer the most.

What should be done?

By all means, keep praying. Call or write your representatives. Fill your churches with vision for a godly America. But please, Christian leaders and pastors, speak up and educate every believer in what is happening to our nation. Call a spade a spade and be plain in your manner of speech. Stop the political correctness. Is it that important if you lose the lukewarm, tepid, and out-of-touch-with-reality church member? And does it really matter if you lose your 501(c)(3) when the global persecuted Church has thrived without such government representation?

It is time to revolt against these demonic ideologies, which are on the verge of bringing judgment down on America if the righteous and every decent American do not act. Again, the words of Martin Luther King, Jr., are fitting for this moment in American history:

"*Cowardice asks the question: 'Is it safe?' Expediency asks the question: 'Is it politic?' Vanity asks the question: 'Is it popular?' But conscience asks the question: 'Is it right?'*"

Remember, evil triumphs when good men do nothing.

CHAPTER 11

THREE MODERN FALLACIES DEFILING THE CHURCH

I heard a popular television preacher recently say this: "If God judges America, He's going to have to apologize to Jesus."

But the Word says: "*For the eyes of the Lord are on the righteous, and His ears are open to their prayers; but the face of the Lord is against those who do evil*" (1 Pet. 3:12).

And this:

"*The Lord knows how to rescue the godly from trial, and to keep the unrighteous under punishment for the Day of Judgment*" (2 Pet. 2:9).

The first fallacy in today's visible, mainstream church world is ignorance concerning God's judgments and even wrath.

FAILURE TO UNDERSTAND GOD'S JUDGMENTS

The aforementioned preacher's understanding lacks balance and the whole counsel of God. He says that Jesus bore our judgment and that, therefore, God will not judge America — or anyone, for that matter. Honestly, this belief system is the edge of universalism.

It says Jesus bore everyone's judgment on the cross, so no one will be judged. Everyone is okay. Everyone will be saved in the end. Actually, it is this popular view that has opened a large door to so much deception in the Church. It breeds a lackadaisical spirit and an absence of holy fear in most Christians. It emphasizes a positional truth at the expense of an experiential truth.

In fact, Romans 1 offers specific proof that America is already under the judgment of God.

"The wrath of God is revealed from heaven against all ungodliness and unrighteousness of men, who suppress the truth through unrighteousness" (Rom. 1:18).

God's wrath is already being revealed. Present tense. In other words, we don't need to wait until the Day of Judgment to see God's wrath. It is being demonstrated now. You need to read the rest of the verses that follow this verse to see this.

"Therefore **God also gave them up** *to uncleanness"* (Rom. 1:24a).

"For this reason **God gave them up** *to dishonorable passions"* (Rom. 1:26a).

***"God gave them over** to a debased mind"* (Rom. 1:28b).

These verses are talking about sexual immorality, specifically the sin of homosexuality and lesbianism. The entire so-called sexual revolution is a product of God's wrath. America has been under the judgment of God for decades! We've praised AIDS victims as if they are heroes, but in actuality, it is the penalty of their sin that they have received (Rom. 1:27).

In fact, when those who practice such things that are deserving of death — and also approve of others who practice them (v. 32) — it is one of God's final signs of His wrath on a society.

SOME EXAMPLES OF THE PRESENT JUDGMENT OF GOD UNDER THE NEW COVENANT

This list does not include the promised, future judgments of God that are also found throughout the New Testament.

1. The wrath of God is currently and continually abiding upon all those who reject Jesus Christ as the Son of God (John 3:36).

2. Ananias and Sapphira (believers) are struck down dead for lying to the Holy Spirit (Acts 5:1-10).

3. King Herod is struck dead by an angel of the Lord for not giving God glory (Acts 12:20-23).

4. Elymas the magician is struck blind "by the hand of the Lord" for being a fraud and son of the devil (Acts 13:8-12).

5. The immoral brother is judged and handed over to Satan for the destruction of his flesh (1 Cor. 5).

6. Believers are judged and become sick, and some even die, for not judging themselves before partaking of the Lord's supper (1 Cor. 11:27-32).

When you take away the present wrath and judgment of God from the New Covenant, you are changing the word of God and removing your name from the book of life and the holy city (Rev. 22:19). You are guilty of creating a god made in your own image and participating in an anti-Christ agenda.

Wake up, Church! What are some of these preachers saying? God's judgment and wrath are already here! Can they escape? Yes, if they turn to God in sincere repentance, they can still receive His mercy and be saved and delivered. But many will not do so.

CROOKED VIEW OF HOLINESS

The second fallacy in much of the Church world today is a total misunderstanding of true holiness. In fact, the Lord told me that there's been a diabolical silence on it.

I believe that restoring the beauty of biblical holiness in the Church is a critical ingredient to healing the moral confusion in our culture. As the Church goes, so goes the world. Our disproportionate view of holiness is one of the big reasons there is so much of the spirit of the world in the Church.

True holiness has gotten such a bad rap and is looked upon with a sort of disdain, as being primitive, outdated, and just not culturally relevant. We need to realize, however, that unsound teaching or negative experiences do not nullify the real meaning, necessity, and beauty of God's holiness.

One of my favorite definitions of holiness as it applies to believers is that it is a moral dedication and a life committed to purity of thought, word, motive, and deed. At the center of that definition is the fact of being set apart or consecrated to God's purposes. In other words, we are not to be conformed to the world's ideals, patterns, or standards, but to God's nature and will.

But even more importantly, holiness has more to do with whom we belong to. To whom do we give our loyalty, love, and allegiance? To be holy means that all we are and all we have belongs to God, not ourselves, and is set apart for His purposes. This is the theme of the apostolic letters to the early churches. How are some believers, even preachers, missing that today?

*"Therefore, having these promises, beloved, let us cleanse ourselves from all filthiness of the flesh and spirit, **perfecting holiness in the fear of God"** (2 Cor. 7:1).*

*"**Pursue** peace with all people, and **holiness**, without which no one will see the Lord…"* (Heb. 12:14).

We are to perfect and pursue holiness.

A distorted view of holiness, or simply the ignorance of it, is clouding our understanding of God's true love. When God is seen as a loving, non-demanding pushover whose love overrides His holiness, whose grace no longer teaches us to deny ungodliness and worldly lusts, then people will live in accordance with that belief and come under the judgment of God. Permissiveness and promiscuity will be prevalent.

This brings me to the third big fallacy I see in the church today, and that is the false concept of the love of God.

WRONG CONCEPT OF THE TRUE LOVE OF GOD

"My little children, let us not love in word or in tongue, but in deed and in truth" (1 John 3:18).

There's a sentimental, mushy kind of love expressed in the Church and in the lives of so-called "Christians" today that falls so short of the real God-kind of love. It is a love not based on truth and deeds.

For example, one of the hot controversial topics today is that of the aforementioned homosexuality. More and more people in the Church world are accepting it and, now, even celebrating it. Entire denominations are now ordaining gay clergy. This is being done all in the name of love. But it is so clear from the Word of God that this is a complete abomination that should have no place whatsoever in the church. There are churches and entire denominations turning into *"synagogues of Satan" "where his throne is"* (Rev. 2:9,13). Doctrines like this are the *"depths of Satan"* (Rev. 2:24).

Does this mean we should stop loving gay people? Of course not. We should love them all the more because they are in grave danger, but we must do so with wisdom, speaking the truth to them. But most people will hate you for it, just as they did Jesus.

"No man was ever more loving than Jesus Christ. Yet even His love made people angry. His love was a perfect love, a transcendent and holy love, but His very love brought trauma to people. This kind of love is so majestic we can't stand it." (R.C. Sproul, The Holiness of God).

You see, love must be mixed with truth and holiness for it to pass the biblical test. As I said, today we are altering the Scriptures because we don't like certain verses that contradict the lifestyle that we or our friends may be living. I knew of a great young missionary in my younger years who labored in the same part of the world as I did whose adult son is now a homosexual. This former missionary/minister recently praised his son for forging his own path and loving those who adopt the same gay lifestyle. Many have removed God's judgments and wrath, holiness, and hell, right out of the Bible. It's one of the signs of these evil last days we are living in.

We may criticize what is happening in the world all we want, but judgment must begin in the house of God if we desire to see His glory and the awakening that many of us have been praying for. Let us remove the evil from us. Let not any form of sexual immorality be even named among us (Eph. 5:3).

"For the time has come for judgment to begin at the house of God, and if it begins first with us, what shall the end be for those who do not obey the gospel of God?" (1 Pet. 4:17).

CHAPTER 12

ALL THAT IS WRONG WITH "CHRISTIAN" AMERICA

This response to a Charisma article I wrote on the liberal-leftist, anti-Christ agenda so accurately identifies the current problem in our nation:

"Millions and millions of liberals are Christians. They read their Bibles. Attend church. Donate to Christian causes. Love Jesus.

"Please, Mr. Farias, I beg you not to divide the Body of Christ over politics.

"Even if you don't love liberals, love Christ, and his church."

FACTS:

1. You can no longer be a leftist-liberal and be a Christian at the same time.

2. You cannot read your Bible with unfiltered lenses and be a leftist-liberal.

3. You cannot attend a church that preaches and teaches the unadulterated gospel and be a leftist-liberal.

4. You cannot love the real Biblical Jesus and be a leftist-liberal.

5. A true-leftist liberal now represents an evil, anti-Christ agenda.

6. I am not dividing the body of Christ over politics, but over evil. As a preacher, I bear the responsibility of exposing the evil in a society and a backslidden church. The light of Christ brings a sword and division (Lk. 12:51-53).

7. I love human beings, even those who are liberal, but I don't love the evil, wicked systems in politics and the world.

8. I love Christ, and my life's purpose is to obey Him. Pleasing Him is far more important than popularity and man's approval.

9. I love Christ's Church and that gives me great cause to prepare her as a bride without spot or wrinkle for the Bridegroom. That is a big part of my calling.

10. Millions of leftist-liberal "Christians" represent the ultimate hypocrisy of American Christianity. It is an evil dichotomy that is de-filing much of the Church and destroying America. Many of these "Christians" will never change, even though God is giving them op-portunities. My hope is now in the remnant people of God to advance His kingdom, while still extending mercy to those headed for selective judgment.

The commentator whom I quoted above saw my article as judg-ment when, in fact, it is the greatest of mercies to warn the deceived and unrepentant.

BOTTOM LINE

Foundational to the real, prophetic gospel, especially as the return of the Lord draws near, is the calling out of God's remnant people from these evil, wicked systems, so that they would not come under the judgment of God. God doesn't judge only individual people; He also judges systems, and He will judge the false-church systems of man. This is a principle of judgment and what I consider to be a plumb line, end-time truth.

"Come out of her, my people, so that you will not share in her sins or contract any of her plagues" Rev. 18:4).

Jesus said in Matt. 24:12 that just before His return, the spirit of this age, which is lawlessness, will cause the agape love of many to grow cold. The aforementioned commentator, who professes Christ, is guilty of such. It's the worst of evils and puts him in a position to be selectively judged for his false profession.

In the American/Western context, lawlessness is now expressed as "tolerance." The commentator espouses to this tolerance gospel by suggesting that my exposing the liberal-leftist anti-Christ agenda makes me loveless toward them, Christ, and His Church. He has been blinded and deceived by the spirit of the world that touts the tolerance gospel that is devoid of all righteous judgment. Whenever you hear the word "tolerance" now, you can be sure that what follows is a sophisticated explanation of why the Bible no longer means what it says. Remember, tolerance is the first step toward compromise.

Please hear me. Church systems that have been erected on the wrong foundation must, according to God's laws, bear the fruit of the unbiblical seeds that have been planted within them. These are false systems that God will allow to continue throughout the Church age, which are the tares that grow up with the wheat, which must reach maturity during the final harvest season.

Another commentator got it right:

"Not many on these comment sections understand the true way to protect a nation. It is dangerous and unpopular, and we have unprecedented freedoms that are slowly being eroded by ideologies that are totally against what God says in His Word."

CHAPTER 13

THE DESTRUCTIVE MIND-SET THAT FUELS EVIL

There's another destructive mind-set in the Church today that has fueled the evil in America. It is simply this: God doesn't care about the Democratic Party or the Republican Party. He doesn't care about politics.

For this reason, many Christians don't vote, and many vote for men and women who hold to corrupt values. And I'm sorry, but many are just ignorant of what is going on in our nation and what is at stake.

Let's make this really easy to understand: How many care about the type of doctor, surgeon, or dentist you have? How many care about the person or people who are teaching your children in school, coaching them in sports, or babysitting them?

Would you feel confident in a dentist's chair if you knew the dentist working on you was an unfaithful married man who has an affair with a new woman every other week? Would you feel secure having open-heart surgery performed by a secret serial killer? Would you feel warm and cozy if a pervert or a child molester was teaching or coaching your child?

Why are we so sensitive when it comes to our family and ourselves personally, but not so much when it comes to corrupt politicians whom we endorse and vote for and who will run our country amok and make horrid decisions that affect us personally for many years to come? Who we vote for has a great trickle-down effect, especially in the 21st century, when everything is so blatant and in-your-face now.

We reached a breaking point in the last election, and we are in the time of the greatest political and moral crisis our nation has seen.

KINGDOM CULTURE EXPOSES DIRTY POLITICS

In decadent times like these, that old devilish compromise and serpentine excuse comes creeping in: "don't preach on politics"; "don't mix politics with religion"; and "God is not interested in politics."

Wrong.

I will preach on politics. I will include sins of the culture and the wickedness and corruption of politics in my preaching — and all the more so because politics has a trickle-down effect that touches each one of our lives. It is my responsibility and duty before God and before the people to do so. The whole counsel of God includes exposing people's sins.

"Herald and preach the Word! Keep your sense of urgency [stand by, be at hand and ready], whether the opportunity seems to be favorable or unfavorable. [Whether it is convenient or inconvenient, whether it is welcome or unwelcome, you as preacher of the Word are to show people in what way their lives are wrong.*] And convince them, rebuking and correcting, warning and urging and encouraging them, being unflagging and inexhaustible in patience and teaching"* (2 Tim. 4:2 — AMPC).

Part of every preacher's calling is to press the influence of kingdom culture on the existing culture, as John the Baptist did.

"So the people asked him, saying, 'What shall we do then?' He answered and said to them, 'He who has two tunics, let him give to him who has none; and he who has food, let him do likewise.' Then tax collectors also came to be baptized, and said to him, 'Teacher, what shall we do?' And he said to them, 'Collect no more than what is ap-

pointed for you.' Likewise the soldiers asked him, saying, 'And what shall we do?' So he said to them, 'Do not intimidate anyone or accuse falsely, and be content with your wages'" (Lk. 3:10-14).

"But Herod the tetrarch, being rebuked by him concerning Herodias, his brother Philip's wife, and for all the evils which Herod had done, also added this, above all, that he shut John up in prison" (Lk. 3:19-20).

If you want to be Biblical, faithful, and true, preach and press the values of the kingdom of heaven upon the existing culture, which includes politics.

Politics can be righteous or wicked. It can be good or evil. It can be moral and upright or immoral and corrupt.

Politics can administer life or death.

Politics can administer God's will for America or an anti-Christ agenda of socialism and globalism.

Politics can administer capitalism and kingdom economic principles or atheistic communism and humanistic socialism.

Politics can administer new covenant kingdom marriage or unnatural perverse same sex marriage and gender confusion lunacy.

Politics can administer God-given inalienable rights and providence or government dominion and satanic agendas to rob Christ and the people of their inheritance.

Politics can administer Christian ideals or Islamic corrupt ethics.

Politics can administer equality or racism.

Politics can administer wisdom or foolishness.

Politics can administer morality or whoredom.

Now tell me that kingdom preaching does not include politics! You cannot get more kingdom than to oppose liberal-leftist politics and the evil agenda of the Democratic Party.

DON'T DIVIDE SPIRITUALITY FROM POLITICS

Can you not see and discern that politicians are given power to make decisions that affect us personally and determine our future?

They will influence not only the way our government runs and the state of our economy and our money, but also our public institutions of learning and Church houses. Most importantly, politicians will legislate laws that will exalt either righteousness or evil in our nation for many years to come.

Somebody will take your hard-earned money and use it for their ungodly agenda. Someone is already spending it and getting richer. Many who will run for office do not care about our national debt; they will create another Great Depression. They want to give away free American citizenship, free American healthcare, and free education to everyone who can break through our borders. And they will make sure you pay for it. How can that not stir you to action?

Worst of all, politicians will enact laws that will use your tax money to indoctrinate your children with homosexuality, transgenderism, socialism, false gods, and false religion. How can you continue to be indifferent?

If politicians and their political parties, the media, Hollywood, and academia can convince people on these issues, then they can convince them on anything else, including the rejection of the gospel. This is the reason many youth abandon Jesus Christ and the Church after they leave home and go to college.

Did you know, based on the politics of Twitter, Facebook, Google and other liberal and Democrat-run organizations and companies, that it's "hate speech" if you say Islam is not a peaceful religion or that homosexuality is a sin or that transgenderism is wrong? But they are perfectly fine with banning Chick-Fil-A at airports or removing a monument cross or a nativity scene at a public place or just harassing Christians. Can you not see that voting for politicians with strong core moral values and truth and righteousness affects you personally, your family, children, and grandchildren? But the change is gradual and so subtle, like the proverbial frog in boiling water. What one generation tolerates, the next generation celebrates. We are seeing it all around us.

Politics and politicians continually make decisions that affect these issues. If you love God and you love people, you will be passionately interested in what values and principles are being legislated by our governmental leaders. This is politics, my friends. How can you say God does not care about politics?

As I examine things in the political realm since Donald Trump has become president, here is something I see. In recent attempts from the Democratic Party to unseat President Trump and run him out of office, I have noticed the dominant influence of the dirtiest politics I've ever witnessed in my lifetime and how the FBI, the attorney general, and FISA court judges are all falling under the sway of this extreme avarice for political power.

We have sunk to new levels of evil and the slimiest kind of wickedness and corruption when you add media power to magnify and propagate political power in order to destroy a sitting president. We have moved further and further away from the position of a party that offers to provide the best leadership to truly benefit the people into a political party that is willing to overthrow its own freedom to be in power. God help us!

We need to be praying and looking to the Lord for the best leader-ship for this country and stop thinking we can do this without Him. This is an early reminder to get engaged in the political process and let the Lord guide you in your vote in 2020 and beyond. Look carefully at your candidate and make sure that what they stand for politically and personally is what best represents your values and the direction you want for the country.

This is not about domesticating or politicizing Jesus into our per-ceived "cause." I am well aware that His kingdom is not of this world, and it is not an either-or polarity. It is a third way. But He loves right-eousness and hates iniquity, and we should live and vote the same way.

As a preacher stated recently, don't fall into the trap of making an artificial divide between spirituality and politics. The devil is intensely spiritual, and he loves to infiltrate and possess media, entertainment, institutions of learning, and politics to promote his evil cause and make the broad road to destruction even broader for our nation's people.

Let's move forward and take the fight to him, and let our salt and light be evident in this most critical midnight hour for our nation.

CHAPTER 14

SHOULD CHRISTIANS BE INVOLVED IN POLITICS

AND VOTE FOR THE LESSER OF TWO EVILS?

*** Mario Murillo wrote this article. Permission was granted to me by Mario to use this article as a chapter for this book. ***

Two dumb ideas are being used by celebrity preachers as an excuse to remain silent when they should be mustering the army of God to do its duty. Because of these dumb ideas, the Church in America is losing influence every day. These dumb ideas have produced a confused view of the duty of the body of Christ.

These ideas are putting the Church back into Obama-era apathy at the worst possible time. Think of what is at stake. The Supreme Court, the economy, national security, and everything we hold dear will be lost. Everything Trump tried to do will vanish in an instant. The floodgates of immorality will open.

Here are the two boneheaded ideas that are being taught in many churches:

1. All government is from God, and we must submit and not mention politics.

2. A candidate must be sinless, or we are choosing the lesser of two evils.

And here are the verses that are misused to justify those two boneheaded ideas:

Romans 13:1 "Let every soul be subject to the governing authorities. For there is no authority except from God, and the authorities that exist are appointed by God. 2 Therefore whoever resists the authority resists the ordinance of God, and those who resist will bring judgment on themselves. **3 For rulers are not a terror to good works, but to evil.** *Do you want to be unafraid of the authority? Do what is good, and you will have praise from the same. 4 For he is God's minister to you for good. But if you do evil, be afraid; for he does not bear the sword in vain;* **for he is God's minister, an avenger to execute wrath upon him who practices evil."**

Let's examine these two ideas:

1. It's dumb to say, "Stay out of politics, and submit to government, no matter what." No sane Christian believes Hitler was God's will for Germany. God raised up the nations of the world to bring divine retribution on Hitler. God works through people to restrain evil, and that is also the duty of the Church.

"The authorities that exist": This phrase means authority from God, not rogue authority. Satan is rogue authority. God has always counter-balanced the threat of tyranny by raising up His chosen authority. That is what is meant by "God's minister to execute wrath."

Moreover, it says, "No ruling authority from God is a terror to good works." God's chosen rulers do not persecute God's people. They do not enact laws to ban the Gospel. So, what do you call authority that is a terror to good works?

German believers abused these same verses to justify their apathy. Dietrich Bonhoeffer could not open the eyes of the German church to the horrors of Hitler. His radio addresses warned Germany. He blamed their inability to discern evil on the then current heresy of "cheap grace" that was accepted by the German Church. They blindly submitted to authority. They rejected his warnings, and the consequence was the bloodiest World War in history, and 6 million Jews were annihilated.

Again, the point is that God works through people to stop evil. The silence of the Church in the face of evil is not noble or virtuous — it is itself evil.

Nations can and do pick evil leaders. Even Israel picked an evil leader: 1 Samuel 8:6 *"But the thing displeased Samuel when they said, 'Give us a king to judge us.' So Samuel prayed to the Lord. 7 And the Lord said to Samuel, 'Heed the voice of the people in all that they say to you; for they have not rejected you, but they have rejected Me, that I should not reign over them. '"*

Obama was never God's choice for America. We have a mountainous stockpile of wreckage to prove it.

When evil reigns, God begins a complicated process of re-establishing justice. Human history is messy, but God is at work in that mess. We want storybook endings, but humanity is complicated. Jehovah works like a surgeon skillfully cutting around vital organs to get at the cancer. Jesus taught a parable about the wheat and the tares, saying that they needed to grow together until the end—otherwise the wheat would be plucked up and lost along with the tares. We have a Biblical mandate to discern between the wheat and the tares, and to get involved in the work God is doing to save our nation.

2. It's dumb to waste your vote because you "refuse to pick the lesser of two evils." You must discern where God is working and support it. God uses flawed people: Daniel was probably shocked to discover that God chose to use Nebuchadnezzar.

Instead of looking for a leader who is without sin, we should be asking, "Where is God working?"

Look at what Paul did: Acts 23:6 *"But when Paul perceived that the one part were Sadducees, and the other Pharisees, he cried out in the council, 'Men and brethren, I am a Pharisee, the son of a Pharisee: of the hope and resurrection of the dead I am called in question.' 7 And when he had so said, there arose a dissension between the Pharisees and the Sadducees: and the multitude was divided. 8 For the Sadducees say that there is no resurrection, neither angel, nor spirit: but the Pharisees confess both. 9 And there arose a great cry: and the scribes that were of the Pharisees' part arose, and strove, saying, 'We find no evil in this man: but if a spirit or an angel has spoken to him, let us not fight against God.'"*

Jesus said that the Sadducees and Pharisees were both evil. So, was Paul choosing the lesser of two evils by siding with the Pharisees? Or, was he discerning where God could work? Right now, it is Trump that He can work with. But Trump needs a Congress *he* can work with. We had better work with God in this next election.

Still don't know what you must do? From Nancy Pelosi to Alexandria Ocasio-Cortez, the Democrat Party, openly embracing socialism, have vowed to open borders, seize guns, redistribute wealth, skyrocket taxes, and force the Church to "evolve." The American Church still does not see the danger, and that, in itself, *is* the danger.

Evil is not hard to spot. It hates Israel, Christianity, Biblical morality, the family, and the unborn. The Democrat Party wears this badge of hate proudly. What else do you need to know?

The two dumb ideas explained above are not scriptural, and they will play directly into the hands of those who would take away our freedoms and our rights. They will forever change

America's system of government. It will be impossible to withstand the wave of falsehood and hatred in the next election if we do not follow the truth of the Bible and the leading of the Holy Spirit. We must repudiate these dumb ideas that are crippling us.

But if we see them for what they are, rebuke them, and submit to the Holy Spirit... even a small number of us can bring about a mighty transformation!

CHAPTER 15

FURTHER PERSECUTION OF JEWS AND CHRISTIANS COMING

Think about how much our country has changed since the turn of the century (millennium). Think about how much it has changed just since Obama was in office. I've got news for you. The rapid changes we have seen in the last few years are not coming to a halt anytime soon. In a word, this rapidity of change will continue to increase and mark these last days before Jesus returns.

At the peak of these changes is the intensity of the persecution of Christians. There is a reason for the great disparity between the media coverage on the massacre of Muslims in places like New Zealand and the killing of Christians in nations like Nigeria. The writing is on the wall. Christians are hated, and that hatred will only increase.

There's also a reason why the larger percentage of the nations despise the tiny powerful nation of Israel. Jews are hated and that hatred will also increase.

"*Then they will deliver you up to tribulation and kill you, and you will be hated by all nations for My name's sake*" (Matt. 24:9).

One of the ways persecution will increase in the West is in the form of spying through artificial intelligence. The same way the Chinese government tracks Christians there and keeps a profile on each of them will also be done in America and the West. All the pieces are in place for this to escalate in the next few years. Christians will be the most targeted, not only by the government, but by private companies as well.

Organizations like Amazon, Google, and Facebook are already tracking your life from the sites you visit to the purchases you make, and their algorithms help companies advertise and market their products and services. They know where you live, and they know your occupation. No harm has been done yet, but that will change as Christians in the West draw the line in the sand between righteousness and wickedness. What has been used for mostly good will now be used for evil as the government will team up with private companies to spy deeper into people's lives. The truly righteous will be prey in that day.

Watch out for more laws to be established through congress that will show partiality and steal Christian liberties. The courts will disregard these liberties and determine more and more what is offensive. Homosexuality, including transgenderism, abortion, and Islam will continue to be at the front and center of controversy as leftists seek to clamp down on Christians, churches, and true conservatives. When anything goes awry, especially in our economy, true Christians and conservatives will be blamed.

LIES

It is obvious that honest journalism is at an all-time low. The media lies. Those who pledge allegiance to Islam lie. Sinners, especially those with their own agenda, will lie. Lying or bearing false witness has been done to God 's people throughout the centuries and was something the religious leaders did to both Jesus (Mark 14:56-59) and disciples like Stephen (Acts 6:13). The same shall be done in ever-increasing effectiveness against true Christians in these last days. The media will take words out of context and pervert what was truly said. Global martyrdom will continue to rise, and we may see it here in the West sooner rather than later, because if you can't change someone's faith, you either persecute them or kill them.

Technology now has the ability to transform any video or audio of a person's words and make it seem as though he is saying words he didn't even say. The general populace will believe it because they are seeing it and hearing it on video. Christians will be blamed for things they never said or did.

NO NEED TO FEAR

True believers in Jesus who are consecrated to Him need not fear when they witness these things coming to pass in greater measure. Those who seek first God's kingdom can be assured of the Lord's care, wisdom, and provision in this hour and experience peace beyond human understanding, while those in darkness shall continue to stumble and be full of fear and great perplexity. Light will dawn on the path of the righteous as darkness and gross darkness fills the land.

These are the days to get your house and priorities in order. These are days of cleansing and consecration. New vows of separation from the things of this world shall be made by many who are presently in darkness or in worldly compromise. The household of faith will become more and more precious to those who have truly forsaken the love of this world. In that day, besides our relationship with the wonderful Lord Jesus, our relationship with those of kindred spirits and like-precious faith will be our greatest wealth. There will be great miracles and divine intervention in the lives of believers who place their trust in the Lord. The coming crisis will only minimally affect them.

However, those who put their trust in the systems of this world will have more heartache and trouble, and for some, this is what it will take for true repentance to work in their hearts and surrender to the Lordship of Jesus Christ.

To be warned is to be forearmed. May wisdom teach us to build our house on the Rock of Jesus Christ. It is only those who prepare for the coming storm and days of adversity and persecution who shall not be shaken.

CHAPTER 16

NOT ENOUGH HATE YET FOR AMERICAN MINISTERS AND CHURCHES

In recent times in high-profile media interviews, too many celebrity ministers have been guilty of blurring the lines between truth and error, right and wrong, and sin and righteousness. Lately it seems that, when put on the spot in a public platform and asked a direct and pointed question concerning the great moral issues of 21st-century America, such as homosexuality and abortion, ministers have turned cowardly and given some yellow-bellied political response. This constant compromising to avoid controversy is creating much damage, not only to the world, which is looking for a clear sound from preachers, but also to believers who have little discernment or are growing tired of ambiguity.

For example, one very influential and popular minister who has millions of followers was asked if homosexuality was wrong, and his general response was that his views were evolving. Evolving? That's like saying the Bible is evolving.

Another well-known so-called "pastor" was asked if abortion was sinful, and he offered this half-baked response: "That's the kind of conversation we would have finding out your story, where you're from, and what you believe. I mean, God is the judge," at which point, the secular audience broke into raucous applause.

When the world claps for you concerning your definition of abortion, I can tell you it was a bad job. You just gave them a license to continue justifying murder of the most innocent and to practice and promote what's convenient. You had an opportunity to allow God to use you to bring conviction, and instead, you offered them false comfort. You had a glorious chance to smite their conscience, and instead, you soothed it. You were given a large platform to smash the godless altar of abortion, and instead, you kept it erect.

The truth is, your ratings and popularity were more important to you than speaking the plain truth with wisdom and grace. You were granted an open door to speak the word of God and please the Lord, but instead, you cowered and bowed down to the fear of man and pleased the devil. I'm sorry, but this is shameful for any Christian, but how much more a minister of the gospel.

In a time of darkness and moral confusion in our nation, you could've brought light and clarity, but you actually contributed to the darkness. In fact, the light you think is in you is not light at all, but it is the greatest of darkness.

"If therefore the light that is in you is darkness, how great is that darkness!" (Matt. 6:23b).

You received your temporal reward — the smile, applause and approval of men. But you lost your eternal reward and favor with whom it counts the most — the Lord and Judge of all the Earth. You are disqualified from being a steward of the mysteries of God.

The Scriptures teach us that if we live godly, we will suffer persecution.

"Yes, and all who desire to live a godly life in Christ Jesus will suffer persecution" (2 Tim. 3:12).

Jesus told us we would be hated by the world. Since the world loves you and claps for you, what does that say about you?

"If you were of the world, the world would love you as its own. But because you are not of the world, since I chose you out of the world, the world therefore hates you" (John 15:19).

Jesus, our Lord and Master, was hated (John 15:18). I don't think many ministers understand that. Read again this penetrating and poignant quote by R.C. Sproul that I've referred to before in this book:

"Holiness provokes hatred. The greater the holiness, the greater the human hostility toward it. It seems insane. No man was ever more loving than Jesus Christ. Yet even His love made people angry. His love was a perfect love, a transcendent and holy love, but His very love brought trauma to people. This kind of love is so majestic we can't stand it."

It grieves the Lord, and His angels bristle at such namby-pamby minister-masqueraders, who will not walk in the Lord's truth and authority. They make the lukewarm and religious crowd happy but less holy. These types of ministers need to be held accountable by someone in their network or eldership circle for misrepresenting the Word of God and making abominable behavior sound so respectful. Either that, or they need to get out of the ministry and be a politician or find another occupation that fits their slick and flimflam demeanor.

When "ministers" compromise to prevailing world culture on a major media platform, I repeat, they need to be called out by someone in their network. Biblical Church discipline needs to be applied. At least two admonitions should be given for repentance, and if they remain unrepentant and without remorse, they should be rejected or excommunicated according to Scripture, and the entire Church world should be made aware of it, until true repentance comes forth, followed by a period of restoration. This way, the leaven of their heresy will not spread.

"If a man is a heretic, after the first and second admonition reject him" (Titus 3:10, KJ21).

The majority of the body of Christ has no understanding of this sort of biblical Church discipline because it is hardly practiced and sorely lacking in most of today's professing Church.

This lack of accountability and do-nothingness is at the root of many of our problems in the body of Christ because of our failure to understand judgment. As one friend of mine said recently, you do not get to talk like a compromising politician about homosexuality and abortion in front of pagans and then act like Paul the apostle on CBN or TBN. Some of these "Christian" talking heads need to grow a backbone, eat some spinach, or something. Forgive me, but we have far too many cowards and frauds who are grossly misrepresenting the Lord.

It is impossible to find any preacher, prophet, or reformer in the Bible or throughout history who has had any real power with God who was not hated or who did not have enemies. When there is little hate, that usually means there is little impact and little power.

My point is, there is not enough hate for American preachers and celebrity pastors right now because of gross compromise. It is one of the greatest indictments against the church in this hour. That has got to change for the moral landscape of our nation to shift and make a serious turn toward righteousness. Lack of persecution usually means lack of power.

Conversely, when preachers are hated for speaking the truth, there will also be more people who honor and receive them because they are hearing a clear sound from them. This will nurture respect for a new breed of minister. In other words, the hatred will increase, but so will the esteem and the honor.

The gospel by nature is controversial and offensive. We must stop removing the offense from the cross (see my book, *The Real Gospel*).

CHAPTER 17

THE TUMULTUOUS 2020's: THE DECADE THE CHURCH GETS OUT OF BED

The reality of a word from the Lord came to my wife Carolyn in another dream just a couple of years ago. Contained within this dream is a vital word for the body of Christ in this hour—both corrective and encouraging that will bring hope to many.

In the dream, my wife was in bed and couldn't get out. The same condition was true for the pastors and church we were ministering for, who also couldn't get out of bed (spiritually speaking). My wife noted that she and these pastors possessed overwhelming strength and needed only to be aroused from their slumber and get up.

A large segment of the Pentecostal/Charismatic Church is slumbering right now — under-utilized, under-achieving in the Spirit, not living up to its potential, power, and effectiveness. But there's a new birthing coming, not according to the old order or planting, but now according to a new God-birthing that will flow from the inward parts of the belly (man's spirit).

"The spirit of man is the candle of the Lord, searching all the inward parts of the belly" (Pr. 20:27 — KJV).

In the dream, my wife was pregnant, and the doctors wanted to perform a C-section and cut her open, but someone said she did not have to give birth the old way, as before. Instead she could give birth the God way, from the inward parts of the belly, signifying in the Spirit. At that moment, beginning from her navel, there was an expansion of her belly that blossomed out.

Interpretation: We have super strength in the Spirit to give birth to a move of God and an awakening, but we need only to arise from our slumber and get up.

SECOND PART OF THE DREAM

The dream then moved to a church service where I was preaching. A group of people sitting in the back of the building were not engaged in the word being preached, but instead were thinking and talking about the outing in a park that had been planned for afterwards. They wanted to play, have social time, and were given to entertainment. Their minds were not on the Lord, and what He was saying and doing in the service.

This speaks of the general condition of many in the Church in this hour. The minds of people are swirling with activity, like tuning into different channels every few seconds, looking for another thrill. It's the nature of the carnal mind which leads to death, while the spiritual mind leads to life and peace (Rom. 8:6).

This is the reason Paul wrote:

"Awake, you who sleep, arise from the dead, and Christ will give you light" (Eph. 5:14).

This verse was written to believers. Apparently, as indicated by the verses immediately preceding (1-13), these believers were walking in immorality, covetousness, idolatry, and such, and Paul was admonishing them not to walk in darkness and in spiritual deadness but in the light. Later on, he tells them to *"be filled with the Spirit"* (v. 18-19) and to *"be strong in the Lord"* (Eph. 6:10).

IT'S TIME TO ARISE AND GET OUT OF BED

It is time to arise, get out of bed, and engage in the Lord's work and agenda. This engaging begins with our communion with God by living a life of praise and thanksgiving, and singing/speaking Spirit-inspired songs from the heart. Read Ephesians 5 & 6 in context. The in-filling we receive will affect our hearts and our lives, and will lead to healthy marriages (Eph. 5:22-33), healthy parent-child relationships (Eph. 6:1-4), and healthy employer-employee relationships (Eph. 6:5-9). We've underestimated the power and impact of a Spirit-filled life according to Ephesians 5:18-19.

I'm a revivalist by calling, but the revival my heart is longing to see is not one that can be captured on social media — but rather one that is lived out in the daily lives of believers, symbolized by a consecration to the will of God, resulting in a life of prayer, fasting, giving, and godly relationships, marriages, and families. There is a divine dissatisfaction working in the hearts of God's true people in this day who are no longer content with the performance and production of professional and sensational ministry, often led by self-appointed prophets and masquerading ministers screaming to be heard and bombarding us with yet another headline of a carnally motivated and fleshly embellished prophecy. Social media oozes with such, and it actually entertains people and stimulates their emotions with yet another ear-tickling yak-and-quack. This has created a vacuum in the hearts of genuine believers for authentic Christianity. This has escalated and is leading us into a current move among the body of Christ for relationship-based Christianity, love, discipleship, and the caring one for another.

What good is it to shout, holler, clap, dance, and hear another sermon on Sunday morning if our daily lives, relationships, homes, marriages, and children are a mess? What good does it do to participate in

Christian conferences and events and listen to the latest-and-greatest teaching or revelation or prophecy if we don't possess godly character and a daily life of communion with God in both Word and Spirit? How will our lives count for eternity if we don't have God's plan for what we are doing?

Let's stop fooling ourselves. Let's arise, and get out of bed, and put on the strength of the Lord, and start living according to the potential and effectiveness that we possess inwardly in Christ.

CHAPTER 18

TIME FOR WIMPY CHRISTIANS TO BECOME COURAGEOUS

No Christian in this country is under the threat of death or imprisonment for preaching the gospel. At least not yet. No one's life is in danger. No one is being beaten, flogged, or hardly even threatened. Yeah I know — a baker and florist, among others, had their day in court in a battle over First Amendment rights concerning serving gay couples, and I'm still not sure how that was all settled. But no one is suffering for the sake of the name of Jesus in the same way the early disciples did. Why, then, is there such a passive posture and a cowardice in the church when it comes to standing for truth, righteousness, and morality in our culture? Why are there so few who are rocking the boat of our sinful, wicked, immoral culture?

Jeremiah said it this way:

"If you have run with the footmen, and they have wearied you, then how can you contend with horses? And if in the land of peace in which you trusted, they wearied you, then how will you do in the thicket of the Jordan?" (Jer. 12:5).

America is still virtually a land of peace, but Christians are slumbering and weary with the weights and cares of the world and such indifference. What would happen if, overnight, we were raided by radical terrorists, who demanded we deny Jesus and join their religion and cause or be executed? What if there was a foreign invasion or military coup from insiders, and our government was suddenly taken over, and a new anti-Christ government was established — and all our freedoms were taken away? It's unlikely at this point — but what if?

C'mon folks — let's be real. Our brand of Christianity here in the West is soft, weak, anemic, and nearly good for nothing.

We resemble the church of Laodicea, who boasted in its supposed blessedness and wealth when Jesus called it wretched, miserable, poor, blind, and naked.

"For you say, 'I am rich, and have stored up goods, and have need of nothing,' yet do not realize that you are wretched, miserable, poor, blind, and naked" (Rev. 3:17).

Many Christians are terrified to stand against the sins of our culture and just tell others it is wrong. In fact, some professing "Christians" will actually celebrate those sins with the world. They will march in gay-pride parades because they say God is love. They will rally for women's rights to abortion because after all, their bodies are their own. They will say that fornication, adultery, and every form of sexual immorality are none of our business, and that we shouldn't judge and yada, yada, yada ...

Adding to their moral cowardice and complete ignorance of biblical standards, these passive "Christians" will defend their personal Jesus and tell others He loves them and understands them. How despicably immoral that is in itself. How grossly deceived they are! How spineless and yellow-bellied these professing "Christians" have become! They've been conformed to the culture and a Jesus they've created in their own image (see my book, *The Real Jesus*) instead of being conformed to the biblical Christ. This makes them twice as much a child of hell as the sinners who commit such sins.

I am not saying our primary responsibility as Christians is to attack the sins of our culture, but where in our society are professing Christians standing against sin and immorality? The world holds up its poster child of sin, and we applaud or remain silent. Anti-Christ laws are legislated, but where is the outrage and the opposition? Where is the strong resistance and defense of the truth? Where is the resolute stand for righteousness and morality?

I am also not saying that our refusal to denounce sin is our greatest problem, but how long will morality and truth continue to give way to an ungodly and evil agenda in our nation? Our faith is either being kicked to the curb, placed in the corners and fringes of society, or just being denied by so many who remain passive and neutral. We've allowed our faith to be cut off from normal life and relegated to our church sanctuaries. In a word, we've been silenced in the public arena. There is a large consensus of Christians who are actually helping our culture build an atheistic society. And we use the secularism in our culture to be secular ourselves. They have influenced us far more than we have influenced them.

BE STRONG AND COURAGEOUS

There is very little strong evidence of Christianity in our American culture, and it's our fault. It is time to heed the Lord's admonition to Joshua.

"Be strong and courageous" (Josh. 1:6a) ...

"Be strong and very courageous" (v. 7a).

"This is my command—be strong and courageous! Do not be afraid or discouraged. For the Lord your God is with you wherever you go" (v. 9).

At least three times God admonishes Joshua to be strong and courageous, and that was after two other admonitions to the same (Dt. 31:6-7). Moses was gone, signifying that strong leaders of the past are gone, and there's another generation who must bear the responsibility of leading God's people in a much more anti-Christ nation and back-

117

slidden church than in years past. It will take great strength and courage.

Because of our lack of backbone and courage, American Christianity is falling off the cliff. We are going the way of the dinosaur if Christians do not become stronger and more courageous in their faith and convictions. We are living in a very pagan culture right now in our nation. Things are so much worse than they seem. The vices, the bondages, and vile filth are expanding at an overwhelming pace. The church is to be the conscience of the nation, but the conscience of so many professing Christians is seared right now.

Our brand of Christianity is lame. It is seen as a nice religion of nice people. A wholesome fanaticism is missing. A life and a vibrancy are lacking. We are too passive and too wimpy. If we want to change our culture, we must come out of our closet of fear and intimidation. Many need to understand that we can be loving and yet fearless and courageous at the same time.

Honestly, we have no need to be fearful and intimidated. As I said, no one is being threatened with their life. No one is being killed for their faith. At least not yet. So, what are we afraid of? The rejection of men? Who cares? Is that really going to matter in the end? There are plenty of others who will applaud you and wax courageous because of your example to stand for truth, righteousness and morality, and share the gospel of Jesus Christ. And God will give you wisdom and grace to love even your enemies.

Let the change begin with you. A little courage will go a long way. And if enough of us wax strong in the Lord and stand tall and courageous, we will, in time, see the change our hearts are longing for.

CHAPTER 19

JESUS TO THE AMERICAN CHURCH:

MEET THE CONDITIONS, AND YOU'LL SEE MY POWER

In December 2001, Sheikh Ahmad al Qataani, a leading Saudi cleric, appeared on a live interview on Al-Jazeera satellite television to confirm that Muslims were turning to Jesus in alarming numbers. "Every hour, 667 Muslims become Christians," Al Qataani stated. "Every day, 16,000 Muslims become His followers, and every year 6 million Muslims decide to follow Jesus."

Amazing! Glory to God! This trend continues throughout nations in the Middle East, in southeast Asia, in North Africa, and a great harvest of souls continues to be reaped in China.

As one of the greatest examples, the nation of Iran, perhaps the world's largest sponsor of terrorism, despite a crackdown on Christians in the land formerly known as Persia, is experiencing explosive growth and harvest. The growth of house churches and secret meetings is staggering. A few short years ago, there were reports of 300,000 believers meeting in secret in Iran, but today, it is estimated that there are more than 3,000,000 believers in Iran (at last count and growing daily). There is widespread disenchantment with Islam, because in Islam, there is no love, no assurance of salvation, and no Fatherhood of God. To them, following Jesus means you receive all these — in addition to spending all of eternity with Him in paradise.

AMERICA

What about America? Why aren't we seeing a move of God and a great harvest like that here? I believe it is because the accountability factor is greater. To whom much is given much is required (Luke 12:48). The nations who are experiencing great signs and wonders, and an unprecedented harvest of souls — as in the aforementioned examples — are those who have not been given as much but yet are experiencing great persecution. Meanwhile, in America, we are drawing back and not walking in the all the light we've been given.

Here again is a great prophetic excerpt from Stanley Frodsham, a contemporary of Smith Wigglesworth that I have referred to earlier in this book:

"With great judgments will I plead with the population of this country (America). Great darkness is coming upon the countries that have heard My gospel but no longer walk in it. My wrath shall come upon them."

And then he prophesied this:

"Before I visit the nations in judgment, I will begin at My house. When I do cause My wrath to come upon the cities of the world, My people shall be separate. I desire a people without spot or wrinkle, and such will be preserved by Me in the time of My wrath, which will be coming upon all iniquity and unrighteousness."

TRUE DISCIPLES SUFFER PERSECUTION

True disciples don't draw back during times of persecution, but the compelling love and reality of Jesus Christ keeps them moving forward. In America, our materialism keeps us at ease. We must understand, however, that comfort and convenience are not the marks of true disciples and moves of God we see in Scripture and today in other nations. There is a price to pay.

Some might ask, "What then do we do—try and receive persecution?" The Bible tells us that the godly shall suffer persecution (2 Tim.

3:12). If you live right, persecution will come. Our problem is that we try to make a good showing in the flesh so that we won't suffer persecution that comes through the cross of Christ (Gal. 6:12). If more believers in the church in America would simply live godly lives and preach and live the cross, trust me — persecution would manifest.

Listen to the wise words of evangelist Maria-Woodworth Etter, who walked in great power and whose ministry manifested phenomenal signs and wonders right here in America more than a century ago.

"The mistake many of us make is to let the persecutions, and threatenings and rage, and the powers of this world scare us and frighten us. We are not prepared to suffer. We don't trust God and go to Him to vindicate His work for us. We too often draw back or compromise and "use wisdom" of the wrong kind, and are just as well satisfied when the power of God is not manifested so much, and the nice, quiet, eminently respectable modern Christians are not offended. We should be praying and looking for God to work more and manifest His power more. To draw back is not pleasing to God, and therefore, the marvels and miracles, the manifestations of His presence and power are, to a great degree, lacking. Let us go forward. Meet the conditions. Come at peace with all the brethren with love for God and man. Come with the desire that Jesus may be glorified. Meet together in one accord."

What a word of wisdom for the hour we live in!

The conditions are humility, repentance, and prayer, a love for the brethren, and all mankind, and a desire to see Jesus glorified. Many believers know they are not living right, not obeying God in fullness, and drawing back from a truly consecrated walk, and so their conscience is unclean and defiled. They have no confidence and assurance before God and therefore cannot walk and act in faith. As a result, many prayers go unanswered.

ARE YOU PLEASING GOD?

Enoch of old had this testimony that he pleased God (see Heb. 11:5). Paul also made this his life's quest. *"Therefore we make it our aim, whether present or absent, to be well pleasing to Him"* (2 Cor. 5:9, NKJV). Jesus did everything to please the Father (John 8:29). Without faith we cannot please Him (Heb. 11:6), but without obedience, our faith is dead.

"My little children, let us not love in word or in tongue, but in deed and in truth" (1 John 3:18).

"By this we know that we are of the truth, and shall reassure our hearts before Him. For if our heart condemns us, God is greater than our heart and knows everything. Beloved, if our heart does not condemn us, then we have confidence before God. And whatever we ask, we will receive from Him, because we keep His commandments <u>and do the things that are pleasing in His sight.</u> And this is His commandment: that we should believe on the name of His Son Jesus Christ and love one another as He commanded us" (1 John 3:19-23).

As we walk in love and obedience to the light and knowledge we've been given, we will have a clean and undefiled conscience. It is then that our confidence and assurance before God will be strengthened. Our faith will then take hold of God, and we will begin to see answers to our prayers. His power will flow in you and through you. He will infuse you with fresh courage and boldness, and you will bear witness with signs following of the unmistakable evidence of the resurrection and reality of Jesus Christ. Fear and conviction will fall on the unbelievers.

"Meet the conditions," says the Lord, *"and you will see the increased manifestation of My power."*

CHAPTER 20

THE TUMULTUOUS 2020s:

THE DECADE GOD'S UNDERGROUND CHURCH ARISES IN AMERICA

Someone recently asked me what I see for America and the Church's future. Right now, I am seeing the beginning and mushrooming of an evolution of sorts and a paradigm shift concerning both the nation and the Church. A paradigm shift is defined in The Cambridge Dictionary as "a time when the usual and accepted way of doing or thinking about something changes completely." Spiritual paradigm shifts are found throughout Scripture, and our time is no different. The Church has created usual and acceptable ways to conduct things, and God is looking to change it completely.

The coming spiritual paradigm shift is being produced by an increase of intimacy with the Lord that brings with it a call to holiness and consecration. This is an inward work as we surrender to His will and His heart. But this will result in a rising glory in God's remnant people that is both infectious and countercultural. We cannot fully grasp the vision of this last days glorious church and the greatest harvest of ingathering of souls ever seen. We have no grid for it. Great power will come with it, a power greater than anything the Church has witnessed over the last 2000 years.

Right now, something is brewing quietly underneath the surface like a tsunami building strength out in the middle of the ocean before it rises and hits land with great force.

Here's a powerful word from the Spirit of God that I've shared before in a couple of my other books:

"Do not look at the TV and larger media ministries to try to un-derstand what I am doing in my body today. They have a part to play, but they are the visible-to-the-eye veneer of the body that people see. Those who are carnal and immature see the outward appearance and are impressed, thinking that these are the height of ministry and where the Spirit is concentrating today. But they are mistaken.

"See what I see: many small churches and ministries investing in relationships, walking in love, pouring their lives into each other; this is where the Spirit is moving today. There is a revolution taking place in my body, a revolution of relationships, discipleship, and love. This will affect whole communities and economies." —John Fenn, Church Without Walls International

I believe God is giving the Church — and, subsequently, the na-tion — a few more years of grace to repent before a new season dawns. The Church will remain under divine discipline until then, as God awaits an earnest and heart-felt response. He is separating the wheat from the chaff. There must be a greater distinction between the world, the false and worldly Church, and the true disciples of Jesus through the work of the cross. Both His severity and kindness are manifesting simultaneously (Rom. 11:22) as people choose whom they will serve. A large segment of the Church is being upbraided for her worldly ways and worldly thinking, and her departure from the real faith.

God is preparing what I call an underground Church and a lov-ing, consecrated people against a time of both great trouble and great harvest yet to come. This is a necessary work, and more importantly, a manifestation of God's mercy to the masses, because when the Church is judged and cleansed, that is when we have the greatest impact on the world. Conversely, when there is lack of judgment in the church, it means a widespread judgment to the masses and mercy reserved for only a small, righteous remnant.

"For the time has come for judgment to begin at the house of God; and if it begins first with us, what will be the end of those who do not obey the gospel of God? Now 'If the righteous one is scarcely saved, where shall the ungodly and the sinner appear?'" (1 Pet. 4:17-18).

As a nation, America will either rise from its spiritual deadness or become a byword. Although I believe God is using President Trump in amazing ways at this writing, he is not the savior of this nation. Let us not be foolish and misplace our trust. A demonic assault has been un-leashed in our land, and it is manifesting in an irrational hatred to-ward everything that is pure, holy, and right.

Let's not stop watching and praying, because we now have new conservative Supreme Court judges, and the nation seems to be on an economic upswing. Don't be fooled. There are many enemies of Amer-ica, and many are now within the Church. It has become rather obvi-ous that there are those who are lurking in darkness and want nothing more than the death and destruction of the Christian values and liber-ties we hold dear. It is the biggest hurdle to globalism, humanism, and a one-world order.

MANY OF GOD'S PEOPLE ARE YAWNING

Seducing spirits are speaking lies, and doctrines of demons are rampant. Perilous times keep intensifying. Hurricanes, floods and fires rage, and volcanoes are on the brink of eruption. The frequency of the Earth's tremors and quakes is accelerating, too, as creation groans, but still so many within the church seem unfazed. In spite of all these dis-asters and the hatred and demonic assault on our nation, the real spirit of repentance is rare these days. What will it take to wake us up?

"My people are yawning at My intentions and will," says the Lord.

There are still too many hirelings, misguided pastors, and ministers who are engaged in drinking, dealing with various forms of immorality, entangled in materialism, or flirting with some other darling lust. Some are bored in their callings and lack true communion with God. The absence of the presence of God is glaring in many places, and sheep are starving for the true word of life. Holiness has been replaced by hype. Appearance has been substituted for the true anointing.

On the other hand, it's also been very encouraging to witness struggling pastors who are laboring in obscurity, pressing into God in the Spirit and taking an uncompromising stand for the Lord. Still, others are growing increasingly discouraged and compromising for growth, or they're just giving up and quitting. Meanwhile, some pastors of mega-churches who have a platform and means to make an impact on their community and nation have greatly compromised the full counsel of God and grown comfortable and self-congratulatory in their false success.

We need so much fire and holiness in the pulpits of America right now, but much of what we seem to be getting is smoke and noise as men are caught up in their own self-importance and image. We have some of the largest churches we've ever had in the history of our nation and yet the greatest departure from the true faith. What a paradox! Many professing Christians don't read their Bibles any more but trust only in what their favorite elevated preacher says.

And so the moral landslide continues, and anti-Christ legislation keeps forcing its hand in our land, while our more visible celebrity preachers and slick televangelists boast of their empty paper exploits while reveling in their creature comforts and raking in their millions.

I weep at the deception of it all and the many preachers who are actual enemies of the cross of Christ and bound for destruction and perdition.

WHERE IS THE TANGIBLE FRUIT?

Where are the testimonies from these celebrity ministers of massive repentance resulting in genuine conversions of lasting fruit, mighty baptisms of the Holy Spirit, and notable deliverances from those who have death-gripping addictions? Instead, most of American Christianity glorifies the hype of noisy conferences, emotionally stimulating popcorn services, and powerless hipster preachers who never speak of sin, true holiness, or repentance. God has only a faithful remnant who are seeing beyond the surface and who hear the rumblings of a massive change and shaking that is coming.

It's all a numbers game that some of these mega-ministries and churches are playing, and it's the popularity and money that seems to matter most to these men with mega-egos. I'm sure there are some who actually love people and are doing much good, but many of them really have no ground strategy. The small guy who's making a marked difference and labors for souls at a grass roots level is not esteemed nor fully supported.

I know many of my former students and friends who have such a strong anointing to impact our culture, but many in the body of Christ are duped into supporting the popularity of elevated ministries who teach, teach, teach, but can never provide a quantitative account of transformed lives. They have millions of dollars in support but little fruit to show for it. It's time to address this farce and inequality, reevaluate our giving, and direct it toward those who are most worthy.

I know of sacrificial missionaries who work in gospel-starved areas among the unreached, ministries who are saving young victims of sex trafficking, those who are building hospitals for the sick and elderly and orphanages for the fatherless, and Christian organizations who support the persecuted Church and families of martyrs. Most of these ministries operate on such a minimal budget in comparison to others with multimillion-dollar budgets who teach those who've already been taught. As important as teaching is in its proper context, let's be honest with ourselves: We are a teaching-saturated culture with minimal tangible fruit that would include a mighty harvest of lost souls.

And what are we teaching? A sugar-coated, affirming, pleasant, feel-good word that keeps the Church self-centered, anemic, and ineffective while thinking they are in revival. The power of redemption has been removed from the gospel, and our nation is paying for it. I'm afraid the fake love and tolerance gospel has come home to roost.

SOUND THE ALARM

Do I sound like an alarmist? Perhaps, but a loud alarm is necessary to wake up the sleepy, yawning church.

The book of Revelation is alarming to me when I read of the death, destruction, and judgment of the nations. The Bible is not all peace and happiness, dear friends, but full of warnings and casualties. And such an alarm must be sounded in this hour if we are going to give birth to real change.

History remembers mighty moves of God, not mega-churches and mega-ministries who are not known in hell. Are there any great mega-churches and mega-ministries? Perhaps a few, but not many. I'm afraid most of them have only added to the deception, providing an appearance of false success — a facade to hide all that's wrong with the American Church, with most having no real impact on the culture of sin.

May God's underground Church arise in America.

CHAPTER 21

RETRIBUTION TIME OF NATIONS WHO PERSECUTED JEWS IS OVER

My wife received a revelation from the Lord in prayer recently concerning the nations who persecuted the Jews during the days of Hitler, WW II, and thereafter. The Spirit of God showed her that the door for the gospel was temporarily closed in those nations, but that time was coming to an end. He said that the last of that generation has died off and that the time of retribution for those nations was over. We will now see the mercy of the Lord manifest as those nations open wide again for the gospel.

My research shows that the main Axis powers during WW II were Germany, Japan, and Italy, although Italy later reneged and changed their course. The Axis leaders were Adolf Hitler (Germany), Benito Mussolini (Italy), and Emperor Hirohito (Japan). These Axis powers (also known as the Axis alliance, Axis nations, Axis countries, or just the Axis), was the alignment of nations that fought in the Second World War against the Allied forces, which included the United States.

Other Axis nations included Hungary, Romania, and Bulgaria. You will now begin seeing more divine activity in these nations in the years ahead.

Why is this important?

Not only are the sheep and goat nations divided according to the the criterion of how they treated the poor and the least (Matt. 25:31-46), but I believe anti-semitism is also a good test of whether a nation is a sheep nation or a goat nation. Sheep nations are blessed nations. Goat nations are not. There was a certain period of retribution required for the nations that persecuted the Jews, especially during WWII. That time of retribution is closing now.

Other nations have received their last call and will not receive another. I'm not saying that people cannot still be saved in those nations, but it will usually come with a price. What the Lord was revealing in the dream was that the dispensation of what Germany did to the Jews is now ending and that mercy is being extended. Thank God that His mercy will never run out until the end of the Church dispensation, and that, even in the tribulation period, people will still be saved, but in a different way (Rev. 14:6-11).

There's been a release of what was blocked up, and what was a hard place with very little moving of the Lord, is now opening up. In other words, the judgment against Germany is over. There's a harvest coming to Germany, and those being born now who have no history or attachment to past generations are free from that judgment. The same goes for Japan, Italy, Hungary, Romania, and Bulgaria. Look for an increased move of God and a greater harvest of souls being saved in those nations.

There are sowing and reaping laws involving nations and agreements and covenants they've made with devils and with evil. There is a blessing on the nations who bless Israel and a curse on those who do not.

"I will make you a great nation; I will bless you and make your name great; and you shall be a blessing. I will bless those who bless you, and I will curse him who curses you; and in you all the families of the earth shall be blessed" (Gen. 12:2-3).

Just look at some of the Middle Eastern nations. For example, although there is great revival in the underground church of Iran, the nation and its people have suffered for years, as well as nearly every Islamic nation. Wars, civil unrest, murder, poverty, famine, corruption, and failing governments are the rotten fruit of those who reject the gospel of Jesus Christ and persecute the Jewish people.

Even in a small way in America, we have seen this. For example, Henry Ford, the founder of Ford Motor Company, who established his company in Detroit, and purchased his hometown newspaper, The Dearborn Independent, was an anti-Semite. This is well documented. I wonder if the trouble, riots, murders, poverty, and such curses that have been attached to the city of Detroit in recent times are the result of that hatred. Even Islam has infiltrated into that region more so than in most other regions of the country. Dearborn is Islam-infested. Just a thought I have.

Why are regions such as the Middle East, North Africa, and other Eastern nations that were once evangelized and Christianized in the early centuries now infested with bastions of false religion and the worship of false gods? Is even the general hatred and rejection of the Jews worldwide a reaping of their own rejection of Christ? Just asking some honest questions and thoughts I've had.

BRASS HEAVENS

I know that the nation of Germany was shut up from true lasting revival because of their mistreatment and murder of the Jews.

Here's an interesting personal account of what happened to my wife when we were in Hamburg, Germany, years ago. She was awakened one morning at 3:00am to pray. As she attempted to go into prayer, there was no anointing or the Spirit's help for her to do so. The next morning, the same thing happened. You have to know my wife Carolyn; she has an anointing to pray, but she won't struggle on her own without the Spirit's help for very long.

After inquiring of the Lord, He told her that the heavens were like brass in Germany and that believers struggle to pray. He told her that He wanted her to experience that so she could have compassion on them when teaching them on prayer. This was a revelation from the Lord, and it aligns with what the Lord recently showed her about Germany's persecution of the Jews. Well, that time is over now, and a harvest is coming forth in Germany, and in other nations that participated in anti-Semitism during and after the WW II era.

"*Therefore be patient, brethren, until the coming of the Lord. See how the farmer waits for the precious fruit of the earth, waiting patiently for it until it receives the early and latter rain*" (James 5:7).

The latter rain will be poured out in those nations now so that the precious fruit of the Earth — a harvest of souls — may be reaped. Not only upon those anti-Semitic nations, but all over the world, we are coming into the ingathering of the last-days harvest that began to pick up momentum in the beginning of the last century.

What a great time to be alive and be a laborer in the Lord's harvest fields! While America is in the final stages of her last call, other nations that had been closed to the gospel are opening up.

CHAPTER 22

INCREDIBLE 1963 KENNETH E. HAGIN VISION

OF ATHEISTIC COMMUNISM IN AMERICA

Yea, the hand of the Lord was upon me ... the Spirit of God moved upon me ... the voice of God spoke unto me and said, "*Come up, come up hither son of man.*"

I went, as it were, up into the air and stood with Him, the Head of the church, even the Lord Jesus Christ...in the air. And as I looked down upon the ground, I could see as a map laid out before me of the entire nation — all the states of the continental United States. And as I looked, He said,

"*Behold son, and I shall show you that which shall come to pass, and that which the eyes of many shall see. And they shall remember that their ears heard that it shall come to pass.*"

For there came a dark hand up out of the ocean from the east, even from the Atlantic Ocean. It came up out of the sea as a hand, and as it rose up into the air, it became a dark cloud, and it filled the whole atmosphere. Yea, and it swept in like a storm at sea. And I said, "Oh Lord! Oh Lord! Oh Lord! What's the meaning of this?" And He spake unto me and said,

"***Son, that is the darkness of atheistic communism that is sweeping across the nation—even in the minds of men in high places and politicians with great power. And this nation shall not grow stronger, and you shall not have more liberty than you have now, but liberties that you've known and you've seen shall be seized and taken from you.***"

And I looked again, and I could see upon the mountain a blotch, as though a bottle of ink had been spilled and spread out over several states in the south and east. And then I looked, and I could see spots splotched all over the map. I said, "Lord, what meaneth this?"

And He said,

"Communistic inspired hatred among races shall cause greater turmoil than your nation has seen heretofore. Yea, it is not the will of God, but men's hearts are perverse, and they walk without the love of God and seek to have their own way. And so it shall be worse than you have seen."

And I said, "Oh Lord! Oh Lord! Is there a remedy? Is there a remedy? What shall the answer be?"

And He said,

"Evil men and seducers shall wax worse and worse, deceived and being deceived."

And then I said, "Oh, Lord! Do we have nothing to look forward to in the future except the darkness, the blackness, war, destruction, and evil?"

And He said,

"Son of man, forget not your text for you look at the things not seen." (The title of his message was, *"Looking at Things Unseen."*)

And so, then I looked into the spirit realm, and I saw falling upon that mountain a ball of fire from heaven. The closer to the Earth, the bigger it got, and then, when it came to the Earth, it divided into small balls or sparks of fire, and it fell upon men. And I saw an army of men rise up, and it seemed as though their hands were fire. And there sat upon their heads a tongue of fire. (When I first saw it, it seemed like their whole heads were on fire, but it was tongues of fire leaping.) And I said, "What meaneth this?"

And He said,

"Before the worst shall come and the day of darkness encompasses, there will be those who shall go and who shall carry the fullness of My truth and the fire, not only to the states of this nation but to many other places. For there is a work that must be done, first spiritually, before the Lord shall come.

"Now prepare ye your hearts, for the time is at hand, and the beginning is now; ye shall see, and ye shall know, for the hand of the Lord is upon you. And many of you shall be used in these last days and the work shall progress."

If the beginning of the events in this fearful vision was in 1963, where are we now? Friends, I believe we are nearing the fulfillment of this vision, and the return of the Lord.

If things are going to continue to get worse in America, we'd better build some resistance and resilience now and look to the unseen for hope and a divine response.

CHAPTER 23

WE HAVE ENTERED A NEW ERA

The Godhead has been converging the ages for several decades. We are crossing over into a brand new era. We are moving into an era of both great judgment and great glory, cleansing and consecration, repentance and restoration. This convergence has been in the making for nearly 70 years but is now fully upon us.

This new season will lead the Church into a new era, in which she will more efficiently grasp the end time.

Once judgment, thorough repentance, and cleansing runs its' course, the Earth will be overwhelmed by the power and glory of God that shall be in manifestation through the glorious Church. Then the worst shall come, but the true Church will be gone.

We have no guide or grid for what the Lord will do through a glorious end-time Church. The Church has never faced and done what she is about to face and do. Many will be surprised. Hell shall be shaken. Multitudes shall awaken. God's majesty and holiness shall be revealed and stun the world in a time of gross darkness.

'Arise, shine; for your light has come! And the glory of the Lord is risen upon you. For behold, the darkness shall cover the earth, and deep darkness the people; but the Lord will arise over you, and His glory will be seen upon you" (Is. 60:1-2).

The Lord has been preparing His Church for such a time as this, and many will realize that they've not known Him and will awaken to righteousness. His awe shall be in the Church and in the Earth. People will fall on their face and tremble. The harvest will be reaped by a cleansed, consecrated, and flaming-fire Church.

END OF THE AGE

The world is rapidly changing, and the frequency of awe-inspiring and fearful events is fast-moving, with all things culminating in the future rule and reign of Christ. The kingdom without end shall be more prominent and recognizable. Instead of churches being a subculture, the real believers shall become a counterculture. Its government will increase in visibility, and its function shall be heightened through a very radical remnant. The King will present Himself as He really is, and people shall marvel.

We have entered the harvest of the end of the age. The greatest ingathering of souls is just beginning. The greatest move of God we've ever seen in our lifetimes is upon us. The gross darkness that is upon the people will only make the light of God's kingdom appear brighter.

During the time of Israel's greatest apostasy was also the time when the greatest prophets arose and championed God's cause for a return to radical righteousness. Similarly, God is calling many now to herald the truth of the gospel with fresh fire.

The greatest days of Church history are not in our past but in our present and in our future. Believing this will activate your faith and move you into it. We are crossing a bridge, where all the moves and activity of God from past generations will converge. The Holy Spirit is retro-fitting all past outpourings and various anointings, rolling them all into one, and reactivating them for our times.

We are entering into the glorious Church era, which is far different than what the Church is known for today. Jesus will build His ekklesia that will shake the gates of hell. The true Church has never

been built by man. Christ shall define His true Church and further ex-
pose the hybrid empty form of showy superficial Christianity and
dead orthodoxy.

The Holy Spirit is brooding over His people and moving them
into a divine dissatisfaction. There is a hunger among the remnant for
His real glory. Hope is rising and callings are being activated and reac-
tivated, and many more will now come to repentance and voice their
faith.

CHAPTER 24

CONTRASTING AMERICA NOW AND THEN:

A FRIEND'S EXPERIENCE IN COOPERSTOWN

This article was written by my friend and cultural commentator Larry Tomczak, who also gave me permission to include it in this book.

I just returned from Cooperstown, New York, home of baseball's magnificent Hall of Fame and Museum honoring the game's legends like Babe Ruth, Joe DiMaggio, Ted Williams, Mickey Mantle, Hank Aaron, and Cy Young. It was like entering a time capsule going back to the America many of us grew up in that has been significantly lost.

Cooperstown is as picturesque today as when James Fenimore Cooper described it over 150 years ago in his classic *The Last of the Mohicans*. It is a small town of unimaginable quaintness but also a platform hosting tens of thousands weekly who come to this village and live out a way of life that typified America not that long ago.

Near the Hall of Fame is an expansive, beautifully manicured "field of dreams" complex of 22 baseball diamonds. They're complemented by dozens of dormitories housing 1400 12-year-old boys with their coaches/dads from over 100 cities across America for a week at a time. Each summer this is repeated for 13 weeks with hundreds of thousands of families, friends, and relatives also attending.

There is an opening ceremony that is an extravaganza remindful of the Olympics. The teams play one another in a well-organized tournament that leads to a final "World Series." Special awards are given for deserved achievement, with a closing ceremony featuring a memorable fireworks display. Word is out that Disney is interested in adding this enterprise to its fold.

My grandson never played baseball or even heard of the game until he became one of three adopted boys in my son's family six years ago. Last week he slugged three home runs the final day, and their team finished 15th out of 104 teams.

I cheered wildly at seven exciting ball games and lost my voice midway. The athletic part of the Cooperstown experience was impressive to the max, but this is not what struck a chord with me as I strolled the grounds for seven days.

FIVE CHARACTERISTICS OF FAMILY FRIENDLY WHOLESOMENESS

My extremely positive experience at Cooperstown was a throwback to my childhood growing up in the early '60s. Five characteristics I witnessed are typical of what life was like in America prior to the catastrophic upheaval of the late '60s.

1. TRADITIONAL MORAL VALUES

I witnessed no profanity, pornography, raunchy T-shirts, immodest dress, drugs or drunkenness, inappropriate sexual behavior, homosexuality, or transgenderism.

2. TRADITIONAL FAMILY VALUES

Everywhere I went, I saw fathers and mothers and children together. I observed men of "steel and velvet" leading their families, loving their wives, and mentoring their sons; mothers supporting and nurturing those in their care; sons and daughters respectful to parents and the governing authorities.

3. PATRIOTISM, GRATITUDE, AND HONOR

The manifest respect and appreciation for parents, coaches, country, the American flag, the National Anthem, military, senior citizens, veterans, and even umpires (over 100 served as volunteers) was a sight to behold! Congratulating victors after games, emphasizing teamwork and refraining from criticizing and complaining was both refreshing and inspiring.

4. UNITY, ORDER, AND OBEDIENCE TO RULES AND REGULATIONS

Instead of lawless, "nobody tells me what to do," prideful attitudes, we enjoyed the peaceful atmosphere accompanying self-controlled and well-disciplined children and adults. Respect for the "rule of law" was obvious everywhere in a town with a steady stream of traffic, and on the litter-free grounds with thousands going to and fro.

5. HUMILITY, SERVANTHOOD, AND UNSELFISHNESS

Leaders at Cooperstown exemplified and encouraged parents and coaches to fulfill their responsibilities as humble servant-leaders — not as insecure, demanding bullies. A quote from one of baseball's first black players on a national team, Jackie Robinson, was especially apropos, "I was told of the persecution I would face, but I determined to practice self-control."

My experience at Cooperstown was a stark contrast to the "progressive" vision for America which millions watched being promoted at the recent Democratic presidential debates. I was aghast at the antagonism, anger, arrogance, and absurdity on display. These left-ist-leaning leaders are deadly serious about their intentions. The "progressive" ideas they promote result in the destruction of traditional marriage and family; celebrate perversion as "pride"; foster the demise of The Boy Scouts of America; engender the corruption of journalism and the collapse of "freedom of speech," "due process," and "innocent until proven guilty"; encourage pornography, promiscuity, and lawless illegal immigration and drug legalization; unfettered taxpayer-funded abortion; push physician-assisted suicide, and numerous other initiatives and entitlements that would bring about our demise and bankrupt America.

It's time we collectively declare "enough is enough" and recapture the America we've known and loved.

Is it possible? Can we revive our roots and elevate our vision to that of America's godly founders whose pledge was, "for the glory of God and the advancement of the Christian faith."

Here's the deal: Everything starts as we turn back to God and remember what America was like just a generation ago, when we united together on a field of dreams that can once again become reality in our time.

CHAPTER 25

WE NEED A COURSE CORRECTION

I am just now understanding some things that I couldn't years ago. Then I remember trying to share my heart for holiness with some Christian friends. I'd preach strong, raw messages in churches without ever smiling. It was like trying to drive an armored truck over a stick bridge. People accused me of being too hard and too heavy. Their bewildered look would be best described by the robot that appeared years ago on the show, *Lost in Space*, who would often say, "This does not compute!" But I voiced the robot's other notorious cry, "Danger, danger!"

They didn't really believe the state of affairs in the Church was that bad — or at least not as bad as I was saying. Of course, in my immaturity, my approach was not the best. But what I didn't understand back then was that it was really much worse. In hindsight, it is obvious to see now how a careless and casual sowing in years gone by has, in many places, resulted in the reaping of some pretty rotten fruit. I think time and history have borne witness to this fact: in times of prosperity and well-being, the general populace, including the complacent Christian, will hardly believe warnings of impending danger. Similarly, trouble across the ocean seems so far away. We muse and rationalize, saying, "It could never happen here."

Take the example of the *Titanic*. Who would've believed the unsinkable could sink? The impending danger was infinitely greater than any of the passengers could've ever imagined. Even after it smashed into the infamous iceberg, some still disbelieved the mighty Titanic was really sinking. The unwise captain failed

to heed sound judgment. Captains from other passing ships also failed to respond to signal calls for help. The entire tragedy could've been avoided. All that was needed was a simple course correction.

In many ways, America, among the nations, has been like the mighty Titanic. For a long time now, we've needed a serious course correction. Does God hold the Church accountable when a nation sinks into the deep, icy waters of decadent sin and immorality? When its own recent presidents and many governmental leaders symbolize such? Are we accurate in our reasoning to say that an earlier course correction in the Church would've perhaps and maybe undoubtedly avoided the imminent danger our nation now faces? If captains of the gospel ships we call "churches" and "ministries" would've heeded the warnings of scripture and lessons of history, course corrections could've been made.

Ah! But where were the trumpet voices of the prophets? Where were the sounds of alarm and war? Who was calling the Church to arms? Ah! But we were on the mighty *Titanic*, and the Christian life was, for many, one big, happy party. And what of our mighty, trusted captains? Many were just happy to have us on board. Perhaps only a small remnant who were at the helm even detected that a real course correction was necessary.

In good times, indulgent souls tend to become hardened and develop a false sense of immunity to anything that upsets their earthly security and cozy existence.

This hardness and insensitivity is usually sure proof of their idolatry. Israel was notorious for disbelieving and persecuting the prophets. "But the Church is in revival now," some would say. A few may be in revival, but can you count the ones who aren't? A few are holy and passionately in love with Jesus, but can you count the ones who aren't? A few are ready for hard times and the judgments of God upon the Church and the nation, but can you count the ones who aren't?

SOMETHING HAS TO CHANGE

At critical points in history, great course corrections have been called for. We call them "revivals" and "outpourings" that God has ordained to reverse the process of moral decline and degradation. With great momentum, revivals can turn into mighty awakenings, which change the course of history by altering the course of nations. The Church has always been one generation away from extinction. If not for these merciful and mighty moral course corrections, the Church would undoubtedly fade into oblivion. The next few years in America may determine her ultimate destiny. An awakening or anarchy (or both) will be her fate. One thing is for sure: something has to change.

I know that there are some who will staunchly come to America's defense and question God's displeasure with her. "After all," they will say, "there are millions of Christians in this nation." That is exactly my point. With these supposed millions of Christians, why, I ask you, have we not made a definite, resounding impact in turning our nation around? A strong Church will have a phenomenal effect on any nation. There are even some among us who still insist on calling America a "Christian" nation. They are greatly deceived.

When multiple battles have been lost to reinstate school prayer, or defeating the abortion industry, you can't tell me that America is a Christian nation. When half the nation now believes in same-sex marriage, America is far from being a Christian nation. There are many other characteristics and statistics that clearly prove that America is Christian only in profession, but not in practice (refer to my book, *The Real Salvation*). Clearly, "*the line is blurred; justice is turned back,*

146

truth is fallen in the streets" (Isa 59: 4, 14-15,) because the Church has not lifted up the standard. And when she has tried to, she has failed, because the world does not respect her. A lack of character, wisdom, fire, and power has made us blend and bland. All we do different than the world is talk.

By now, you ought to be able to tell that God has inflicted me with a divine dissatisfaction. **In order for the Church to really *arise,* I believe she needs to first be *aroused.* Before a war becomes physical, it is first spiritual. Those who are casual in war time irk and disturb those who are vigilant. Indifference in life-and-death situations is all the enemy needs to advance. We need to regain the battle mentality and fighting spirit that formerly were so depictive of the Christian life.**

But how can we fight if we don't believe enough in the cause for which we are fighting? Fun, food, and fellowship is the only brand of Christianity some believers have ever known.

SOME CHURCHES NEED TO REINVENT THEMSELVES

Some churches need to reinvent themselves. Never have I seen less evangelism and less effective discipleship than in the churches who pride themselves in being a New Testament church. We have among us many doctors of doctrine but few preachers of power. We have much monotone but little fire. We have many eulogists but few true evangelists — many speakers but so few soul winners. We have many teachers but not many true fathers. We have many meetings where we hear music and sing songs, but so few where we hear groans and loud weeping for the lost. Whatever happened to having faith for lost souls which works by love (Gal. 5:6)? Real faith has humans as the object of its love. A drug addict will find a way to get his drug. Strong love will find a way to reach its needy subjects. Jesus was moved with compassion (Matt. 9:36).

More fun, more food, and more fellowship is not what many of us need right now, unless, of course, it is somehow linked to winning the lost and making disciples. We don't need fads that come and go. We need fruit that remains. More teaching will help only the doer — not the hearer. More fire, more focus, and more fruit are what we need.

Many churches need a course correction. Please allow the grace of the evangelist in me to speak to you right now. Here are a few proposals I would like to make to leaders, ministers, and all saints:

1. Don't get good at what you're not supposed to be doing.

Too many of us are a hundred miles wide and one inch deep. We do a lot of things good but not many excellently. It's time to do some serious evaluation. How many new converts are being added to the kingdom? How many are being discipled? Who are you currently believing, praying, fasting, making intercession for, and lovingly sharing your faith and life with? How many people are really being discipled and not just taught? Who are you currently discipling?

Here is the course many must now take if they are to see more fire and more fruit. Convert more church events into opportunities for evangelism. Convert more doctrine into discipleship. Teach them to observe what Jesus taught (Matt. 28:19). Go back to the gospels. Constantly evaluate everything you do by the great commission — evangelism and discipleship.

2. Water seeds, not weeds.

Weeds are things that don't work or don't matter. We've all heard the saying, "Don't sweat the small stuff." Don't let activity and schedule determine your strategy. Don't immerse yourself into things that rob you of your time with God and with your disciples. Guard your rest, energy, and creativity. Weeds are things God never told you to do and which only rob you of rest, erase your energy, and kill your creativity. On the other hand, seeds are things which are stamped with eternity. They focus more on people rather than programs. Get rid of everything that hinders true kingdom increase.

3. Develop a passion for prayer and for souls.

This should've been listed first. You won't do much without passion. If you're not burning up with a vision for souls, you will affect very few people dramatically and permanently. This is the real reason why men falter and fail. Instead of burning up, they're burning out. Instead of getting fired up, they're getting tired out. Instead of moving on and moving up, they're moving down and moving out.

Find things that ignite and feed your passion for prayer and lost souls. Read a good biography of a man of God who helped many find Christ. Read good books on holiness, prayer, and revival. Feed constantly on the gospels and the book of Acts. Read the Bible on your knees, and ask God to break your heart with the things that break the heart of Jesus. Go find somebody in pain, and bring healing to them. Find the hurting, and encourage them. Seek out the last, the least, and the lost, and make their day. It's in the going — as in "go ye" — that your passion will always be preserved. The way you keep it is by giving it out.

4. Don't separate, but incorporate soul-winning into church events.

Pastors, cater some of your services just for the lost. I think it would help many churches to have an extra special salvation Sunday once a month, or at least once a quarter. Teach your people constantly to love the lost and to reach them. Within the confines of their own personality, encourage every believer, young and old, to befriend sinners and win them to Christ. Instead of posting up a barometer to gauge building-fund giving, put one up to gauge the number of souls won to Christ. Encourage and disciple believers by precept and example in the art of prayer and intercession, and winning and discipling the lost. Make the lost your special guests at church functions such as picnics, holiday events like Easter and Christmas, and men's and women's nights out. This is the real reason why we have fun, food, and fellowship.

5. Lastly, scout out a good evangelist who can help you.

Find one whom you know and can trust that is not just interested only in promoting his ministry or getting an offering, but who really has a passion and a faith for seeing lost souls saved. Personally, I can recommend several good ones. Remember also that winning the lost is not the only function of the evangelist. Contrary to modern Church thought, the primary function of every evangelist is to produce other evangelists and a spirit of evangelism in the church.

At this writing, we are nearing the decade of the 2020s, and by the time some of you read this, we may already be there. The mighty *Titanic*, symbolic of our nation, is sinking quickly. Let us save as many as we can who are drowning in these turbulent, icy waters. Soon the devil may make it a crime to do so.

May God bless you with a broken heart for the lost, and may He give you true kingdom increase. That's the most effective way to change a nation — one soul at a time.

CHAPTER 26

THE CHURCH MUST FIND THE RADICAL MIDDLE

I've often wondered how some groups of people can live a lie so full of zeal, devotion, and commitment, while many in the church live the truth so poorly, purposelessly, and with little zeal and commitment.

For example, Islamic terrorist groups' commitment to a dark and violent cause is often so much greater than the Church's commitment to the truth. They are the product of a message and a mandate that inspires such passion in them, while our gospel produces passivity, powerlessness, and a general lack of zeal and commitment.

Why does their message produce radical disciples for their counterfeit cause, while ours falls so short for the greatest cause ever known to humanity?

Could it be that we are preaching the wrong kind of gospel, thus producing the wrong kind of convert?

Here are the two kinds of gospel I hear in the West:

1. Accept Jesus and go to heaven when you die.

Although true, this gospel falls desperately short of producing passionate, whole-hearted commitment and radicality in its converts. Today, in the West, a church "altar call" (if they even have one) often consists of the pastor requesting for every head to be bowed and every eye closed while they ask for a show of hands raised by those who want to "accept Jesus." That is so very Western, because an Easterner would never think they have the privilege of merely "accepting" the

King into their lives. Instead, they would give their lives to the King, humbly asking that He accept them.

Two minister friends of mine were having lunch one day. They were talking about some of these differences between Western and Eastern thinking, and one friend mentioned a ministry trip to India that he'd been on and what one of the Indian pastors had said.

"You in America preach a different gospel than we do in India," the Indian pastor said. *"You preach that if you accept Jesus, He will heal your family, He will bless you with money and give you more, and He will heal your body. You will be blessed if you accept Jesus. But, in India, we preach that, if you believe in Jesus, your family may reject you, you may lose your health, you may lose your finances, and you may lose your life."*

The West invites Jesus into their already-busy lives, while the East gives their whole life to Jesus to the point of immediately being willing to die for Him if called upon to do so. The West doesn't understand Jesus is a King, instead, we think of Him first as a friend, one who is on our side to improve our life and make us prosperous.

2. Come to Jesus; be like Him, and make the world a better place.

This second kind of gospel appeals especially to the younger generation, as many of them have a passion for making the world a better place through promoting and supporting good causes and being engaged in social activism. They idolize globalism and a superficial love and peace between all men and races.

This gospel is a nice gospel, but the problem is that it is more social than spiritual. It performs acts of kindness and treats people with courtesy and respect, which is noble, but it never preaches the gospel with zeal and power. There is an entire generation that is being bred to these ideals.

The Lord Jesus Christ is not fully represented in either aforementioned group.

Jesus does not want to be "accepted." He is not suffering from loneliness and rejection. He does want to be an addition to or a new-and-improved edition of your life.

When it comes to politics, He is not a globalist or a nationalist. He is not Republican or Democrat. He is not necessarily conservative or liberal, or right wing or left wing. He is not a social activist, or an advocate of justice. When it comes to religion, He is not Catholic or Protestant or anything else.

Who is He then?

He is the holy and mighty Son of God. He is the glorious and majestic King who has come to take over and establish His own kingdom.

Jesus lives in the radical middle.

The above versions of the gospel are not the full gospel. There is nothing in it that moves me to sell everything and follow Jesus. A wholesome fanaticism and fiery zeal is missing. The Church must find the radical middle.

RIGHT WING, LEFT WING, OR THE RADICAL MIDDLE

In Jesus' day, the Pharisees were the conservatives, and the Sadducees were the liberals; both constantly challenged Him to take sides, but He never did. He never responded as they wanted Him to to implied questions or suggestions such as, "*By what authority do you do these things?*" or "*Is it lawful to pay taxes to Caesar, or not?*" Such are the political talking points many believers often argue today on social media.

As we soon head to another presidential-election season, is our hope being placed too much on the political process to bring forth righteousness, truth, and morality in our nation? Are we sitting at Caesar's table to gain influence in effecting laws that will bring the kingdom of God to the Earth, or are we really trusting God?

Not only did Jesus walk in the radical middle, but in days of old, Israel's call was to be the same. In the midst of a dark world and the various political perspectives of that day, Israel was to be a light among the nations for all to see. They were to provide a better hope and a better place for the manifestation of God's glory for people to find fulfillment in.

Such is the highest purpose of the Church today. Through the directives in the New Testament, we are to be a place of love, power, morality, truth, and righteousness. We are to be that city set on a hill who exemplify the higher ways of the kingdom of God. We are to set the example of how to live in love, peace, and unity among one another and manifest the glory and power of God.

And as we fulfill this purpose, we become the people of the radical middle, who position ourselves to be not only the conscience of the nation(s)—but a powerful, prophetic voice and living testimony to all.

The radical middle does not say to the homosexual, "Go back to your closet." Instead, it says, "Come out of your grave!"

The radical middle does not say, "Make America great again." Instead, it says, "Make Jesus Christ and His Church great again!"

Our kingdom cry should be far greater than our nationalistic cry. This will be so only when we find the radical middle. More than making America great again, our high calling is to make the Church great again by making Jesus great, and fulfilling kingdom purposes.

"Now when Joshua was by Jericho, he looked up and saw a man standing in front of him. In His hand was His drawn sword. Joshua went to Him and said, 'Are You for us or for our enemies?'

"He said, 'Neither, for I am the commander of the army of the Lord. Now I have come'" (Josh. 5:13-14).

The commander of the army of the Lord was not for Israel or its enemies. He didn't come to take sides. He came to take over. He came to command His army and to establish His kingdom, which is built on truth and righteousness.

Let us move according to the Lord's command and not our own agenda. He will always stand for truth, righteousness, and justice, for such is the foundation of His character and throne (Ps. 97:2), and it's His rule and reign that we must have the greatest passion for.

Remember that political kingdoms are temporary and will soon cease, but of the increase of His government and peace there will be no end (Isaiah 9:7).

A PROPHETIC WORD FOR THE CHURCH BY LANCE WALNAU: THE DAYS OF JONAH

Be bold for what you stand for, and discerning about what you fall for.

The Lord is allowing the nation to feel the tremor of shaking to let it know that its foundations are eroding under its feet. God gave us a divine reprieve from judgment when He intervened in our last election. A reprieve is a delay of sentence.

Could the hour of divine mercy, under the era of Trump's Presidency, be running out? His enemies have become so focused and energized and his defenders so intimidated and silenced that one can only wonder if 2020 can be won. Yet even then, we are under a reprieve, and that judgment is not subject to our election cycle. The point is — we do not know how long this mercy will last.

I am hearing God say that this shaking will continue. It will multiply in intensity and will produce an increasing desire for stability and a cry for sanity, but the storm will only increase.

It is as in the days of Jonah. The servant of God was on the ship, hiding out, as it were, and he was going in the wrong direction. Jonah was not only subject to the great storm, but he was the object of the great storm.

Those on this boat today will seek to blame and explain what is happening. They will continue to "cry out to their gods," and, for many of them, it is a political messiah they seek. They will blame this group and that group.

You will not be exempt.

There will be increased hostility against the people of God. It will continue to find its way into the discourse of your enemies, and they will say *you* are the problem. We will become controversial and driven from our hiding. And, indeed, Jonah was part of the problem, but not in the way they were thinking.

The storm grew because Jonah was not doing what he was called to do. He was called to preach and speak and warn the people of Nineveh. But rather than cooperate, he was running from his real assignment and trying to avoid his responsibility. Like so many preachers who are building their audience and expanding their reach to enlarge their own house, we are going in the wrong direction in a time of national crisis.

The truth about Jonah is that he did not like the people of Nineveh. He felt they deserved God's judgment. He did not want to be among them. God, on the other hand, wanted to see Nineveh spared judgment, but that would not happen without a word of judgment and the engagement of His people.

Jonah was cast out of the ship.

For too long, the Church and many recognized-name ministries have been focused on their own business. They say that they are doing what God called them to do, but, in truth, they are self-absorbed. And when I say "they," I include myself in this examination. We have tried to ignore the storm and avoid stormy topics. We have been building *our* house while God's project — His House and the nation — are coming apart.

That is about to change. We're not going to fit in so comfortably in the days ahead. The time of courting the world's approval will soon end. They will no longer be cordial with us. They will cast us out of the ship.

And that is when we will wrestle our way into the repentance necessary to deliver the word we are called to give. Indeed, the wrestling has already begun.

There is no doubt that people are praying. When God's people cry out, God answers by sending a messenger.

I don't know what big fish God is preparing, but I do know the fish is a picture of the place where we end up as we come to terms with obeying God. And miraculously, the fish will position you to enter Nineveh.

The storm is real, and the reprieve is real. Mercy wants to avoid judgment, and this moment and decade are as the days of Jonah.

CONCLUSION

What I love about God's remnant is that they represent the Great Intercessor. It doesn't take a prophet to see that America is on the verge of severe judgment and in the grips of doom. But this praying remnant says, "No, Not without a fight!"

With some apostolic reformers and nameless, faceless intercessors who are pure in heart and are driven by the true Spirit of Christ, positive change is still within reach, and the dominion of the Father can be established.

Let that resounding reverberation of the Father's heart ring through the lips of a praying remnant. Let us pray His will, for the Lord delights in showing mercy, and mercy triumphs over judgment.

Let us pray that the consciousness and awareness of America shifts, that repentance is granted to this country, and that the people fall at His feet, so that restoration can come.

God is purifying his pioneers for this, and raising up "agents of change" who are not driven by personal ambition, but they minister to Jesus with a passion for His benevolent and merciful heart. The last days will come, but "we the people" don't have to end in ruin. The Spirit and the bride say "Come."

CHAPTER 27

SHOWDOWN COMING: TIME OF PLAYING CHURCH IS OVER

In a recent interview, a former Texas congressman was asked if he thinks religious institutions like churches, charities, and even colleges/universities should lose their tax-exempt status if they oppose same-sex marriage. Here's his response:

"Yes, there can be no reward, no benefit, no tax break, for anyone, or any institution, any organization in America that denies the full human rights and the full civil rights of every single one of us."

The writing is on the wall. We are at the threshold of a greater persecution of the American Church. The spirit of anti-Christ and atheism is gaining momentum in our nation. The warning signs are in plain view for all churches and ministries to see. If it can happen in other nations, it can happen here. America is not exempt. Could some within our shores in the not-so-distant future be imprisoned or even killed for their faith?

Notice the former Texas congressman didn't specifically include Islamic centers or mosques. Islam kills gays. America nows celebrates gay marriage. Yet most Democrats and even some Republicans are so tolerant of Islam. How utterly illogical and lunatic is that? America was founded on Christian faith and principles that gave us our freedom, but now these evil men desire to enslave us through their anti-Christ and anti-biblical laws.

Furthermore, in a recent debate, some of the Democratic candidates also promised that, if elected, they would do the same and pass a federal law that any church or ministry who taught publicly against the gay lifestyle or same-sex marriage would be stripped of its 501 (C)(3) non-profit status. Among other negative results from this, it would mean that people's tithes and offerings would not be tax-exempt, all special permits for bulk mailing would be revoked, all land, equipment, and housing for ministers would fall under taxable laws, and, in general, this would cause thousands of churches that are already in financial trouble to close its operations (if and when that day comes, we will learn that the Church is not a building — it is people). Again, this kind of proposal might have seemed far-fetched years ago, but the mere fact that there is now discussion and consideration about it, is a sign that it is here. This is the socialist, anti-Christ spirit that is now entrenched in the minds of some of the politicians and universities in this nation.

Their anti-Christ thinking is this: since same-sex marriage is now law, everyone must obey the laws and support this issue. These despicable politicians are no longer hiding their belief that government should exercise control over religion — or, should I say, exercise control over Christ's true Church. Religion is not the threat — the true Church is.

The truth of what Jesus taught is this: They are of their father the devil, liars and murderers, haters of Christ, and of true Christians. They love their own like Islam and false religionists (John 8:44). That is why you never hear cases of discrimination being made against Islamic centers and mosques or Muslim businesses. Gays don't go to a Muslim bakery and ask for a gay wedding cake. Gays don't sue Muslims for discrimination. This world's system is only against Christ and His true Church. Please understand that.

Christ likened the last days before His return to the days of Noah and Lot. In Genesis 19, we see Sodom promoting abominations of old and young men having homosexual relations. Biblical commentaries tell us that, when strangers came to the city of Sodom, the men placed beds in the street, tying the strangers to the bed, and physically abusing them — thus the reason Lot requested that the two men (angels) not go outside the door of his house, as it would be dangerous. America has been doing the same for sometime now. Gay rights, gay pride, gay parades, and gay marriage, and every other kind of perverse thing are legal and celebrated.

TAX EXEMPT STATUS IS NOT A REWARD

Allow me to educate some of these ignorant politicians. The tax-exempt non-profit status actually exists, not for a reward, as some of these loony minds profess, but for humanitarian services to be granted to the poor, needy, and less fortunate. But they are ignorant of their own laws and now want to use them to penalize true Christian non-profits, thus punishing millions from receiving their services, because they somehow believe our faith and holy convictions, which are centuries and millennia old, are discriminatory.

In actuality, they want to reward the 4% LGBTQ community and punish the Christian right to free speech and worship of God. It is now becoming culturally acceptable to discriminate and infringe on the deeply religious convictions of millions of Bible believers.

IT IS TIME FOR FAITHFUL DISOBEDIENCE

Beloved, it is time for faithful disobedience to anti-Christ laws that are under discussion and consideration by our own government. When man's laws contradict divine law, the kingdom of God must follow the rules of heaven and not of men.

But Peter and the other apostles answered and said: "*We ought to obey God rather than men*" (Acts 5:29).

The Medes passed a law that men could not pray to any God in Babylon, but Daniel refused to follow it and prayed three times a day. Another law was passed to bow down before an idol or be burned in a furnace, and three Jewish young men refused to bow. Conviction and faith overruled human laws and agendas that were contrary to God's law.

"Let it be known to you, O king, that we do not serve your gods, nor will we worship the gold image which you have set up" (Daniel 3:18).

These God-haters and evil champions of humanism are desiring to take away the religious freedom and personal convictions of millions of Americans and will use "rules of intimidation" to accomplish their goals. It is a demonic agenda. The true Christian faith and belief system is under assault, similar to how socialist-communist Russia arrested and killed Christians when they came under the rule of ungodly dictators.

These agents of Satan and evil men will wax worse and worse until Christ's coming. They want power and control that will lead to a progressive society totally devoid of God's laws and judgments. To them, the Bible is an outdated book that has no place in today's world. One state has already proposed a ban on using the Bible to counsel any transgender or person living the gay lifestyle.

Listen to me very carefully. We are coming to a showdown that we have never seen before in modern America, and, as it was in the days of Elijah, Christians must decide now whose side they are on. We are coming into a time of faithful disobedience.

"How long will you falter between two opinions? If the Lord is God, follow Him; but if Baal, follow him" (1 Kings 18:21).

THE TIME OF PLAYING CHURCH IS OVER

For the last several years a number of voices have shared much on the dire state of things in our nation and the Church. Some have heeded these messages, but others continue to mock, scoff at, and resist truth on fire. Sadly, many of them will not survive the coming storm.

The time of "playing church" — like little children looking under the heavenly Christmas tree for the next gift — is over, and we've entered into a time where we must put away childish things, and become serious followers of our Master, and understand that the spiritual war we are in is about to intensify.

As I stated repeatedly, bittersweet times are ahead. We will choose our own way. Everything that can be shaken will be shaken as we enter into the times of the fear of the Lord. It is time to awaken from our slumber. You can be awakened with a kiss of kindness or shaken with the Lord's severity. You must choose whom you will serve, for the Lord will distinguish again the righteous from the unrighteous, the holy from the profane, and the serious follower from the fan of Jesus.

Nevertheless, the solid foundation of God stands, having this seal:

"The Lord knows those who are His," and, *"Let everyone who names the name of Christ depart from iniquity. But in a great house there are not only vessels of gold and silver, but also of wood and clay, some for honor and some for dishonor. Therefore, if anyone CLEANSES HIMSELF from the latter, he will be a vessel for honor, sanctified and useful for the Master, prepared for every good work"* (2 Tim. 2:19-21).

He who has ears to hear, let him hear what the Spirit of God is saying to the Church.

CHAPTER 28

AN EXAMPLE AND A CALL TO FAITHFUL DISOBEDIENCE

Following is a letter written by a Chinese pastor on the matter of faithful disobedience and what this all means for the serious follower of Jesus Christ. May his words greatly strengthen your resolve to remain faithful to Christ, especially during times of greater persecution that will come as the return of our Lord Jesus Christ draws nearer.

Editor's note: More than 100 members of Early Rain Covenant Church in Chengdu, China, were arrested beginning Sunday, December 9, 2018. At the time of publication of this translation, arrests are still being made. Among those taken away were Pastor Wang Yi, senior pastor of Early Rain, and his wife, Jiang Rong, who have not been heard from at the time of this writing.

Foreseeing this circumstance, Pastor Wang Yi wrote the declaration below to be published by his church should he be detained for more than 48 hours. In it, he explains the meaning and necessity of faithful disobedience, how it is distinct from political activism or civil disobedience, and how Christians should carry it out.

HERE IS HIS LETTER: MY DECLARATION OF FAITHFUL DISOBEDIENCE

On the basis of the teachings of the Bible and the mission of the gospel, I respect the authorities God has established in China. For God deposes kings and raises up kings. This is why I submit to the historical and institutional arrangements of God in China.

As a pastor of a Christian church, I have my own understanding and views, based on the Bible, about what righteous order and good government is. At the same time, I am filled with anger and disgust at the persecution of the church by this communist regime, at the wickedness of their depriving people of the freedoms of religion and of conscience. But changing social and political institutions is not the mission I have been called to, and it is not the goal for which God has given his people the gospel.

For all hideous realities, unrighteous politics, and arbitrary laws manifest the cross of Jesus Christ, the only means by which every Chinese person must be saved. They also manifest the fact that true hope and a perfect society will never be found in the transformation of any earthly institution or culture but only in our sins being freely forgiven by Christ and in the hope of eternal life.

As a pastor, my firm belief in the gospel, my teaching, and my rebuking of all evil proceeds from Christ's command in the gospel and from the unfathomable love of that glorious King. Every man's life is extremely short, and God fervently commands the church to lead and call any man to repentance who is willing to repent. Christ is eager and willing to forgive all who turn from their sins. This is the goal of all the efforts of the church in China—to testify to the world about our Christ, to testify to the Middle Kingdom about the Kingdom of Heaven, to testify to earthly, momentary lives about heavenly, eternal life.

This is also the pastoral calling that I have received. For this reason, I accept and respect the fact that this Communist regime has been allowed by God to rule temporarily. As the Lord's servant John Calvin said, wicked rulers are the judgment of God on a wicked people, the goal being to urge God's people to repent and turn again toward Him. For this reason, I am joyfully willing to submit myself to their enforcement of the law as though submitting to the discipline and training of the Lord.

At the same time, I believe that this Communist regime's persecution against the church is a greatly wicked, unlawful action. As a pastor of a Christian church, I must denounce this wickedness openly and severely. The calling that I have received requires me to use non-violent methods to disobey those human laws that disobey the Bible and God. My Savior Christ also requires me to joyfully bear all costs for disobeying wicked laws.

But this does not mean that my personal disobedience and the disobedience of the church is in any sense "fighting for rights" or political activism in the form of civil disobedience, because I do not have the intention of changing any institutions or laws of China. As a pastor, the only thing I care about is the disruption of man's sinful nature by this faithful disobedience and the testimony it bears for the cross of Christ.

As a pastor, my disobedience is one part of the gospel commission. Christ's great commission requires of us great disobedience. The goal of disobedience is not to change the world but to testify about another world.

For the mission of the church is only to be the church and not to become a part of any secular institution. From a negative perspective, the church must separate itself from the world and keep itself from being institutionalized by the world. From a positive perspective, all acts of the church are attempts to prove to the world the real existence of another world. The Bible teaches us that, in all matters relating to the gospel and human conscience, we must obey God and not men. For this reason, spiritual disobedience and bodily suffering are both ways we testify to another eternal world and to another glorious King.

This is why I am not interested in changing any political or legal institutions in China. I'm not even interested in the question of when the Communist regime's policies persecuting the church will change. Regardless of which regime I live under now or in the future, as long as the secular government continues to persecute the church, violating human consciences that belong to God alone, I will continue my faithful disobedience. For the entire commission God has given me is to let more Chinese people know through my actions that the hope of humanity and society is only in the redemption of Christ, in the supernatural, gracious sovereignty of God.

If God decides to use the persecution of this communist regime against the church to help more Chinese people to despair of their futures, to lead them through a wilderness of spiritual disillusionment, and, through this, to make them know Jesus, if through this, He continues disciplining and building up His church, then I am joyfully willing to submit to God's plans, for his plans are always benevolent and good.

Precisely because none of my words and actions are directed toward seeking and hoping for societal and political transformation, I have no fear of any social or political power. For the Bible teaches us that God establishes governmental authorities in order to terrorize evildoers, not to terrorize doers of good. If believers in Jesus do no wrong then they should not be afraid of dark powers. Even though I am often weak, I firmly believe this is the promise of the gospel. It is what I've devoted all of my energy to. It is the good news that I am spreading throughout Chinese society.

I also understand that this happens to be the very reason why the Communist regime is filled with fear at a church that is no longer afraid of it.

If I am imprisoned for a long or short period of time, if I can help reduce the authorities' fear of my faith and of my Savior, I am very joyfully willing to help them in this way. But I know that only when I re-nounce all the wickedness of this persecution against the church and use peaceful means to disobey, will I truly be able to help the souls of the authorities and law enforcement. I hope God uses me, by means of first losing my personal freedom, to tell those who have deprived me of my personal freedom that there is an authority higher than their au-thority, and that there is a freedom that they cannot restrain, a free-dom that fills the church of the crucified and risen Jesus Christ.

Regardless of what crime the government charges me with, what-ever filth they fling at me, as long as this charge is related to my faith, my writings, my comments, and my teachings, it is merely a lie and temptation of demons. I categorically deny it. I will serve my sentence, but I will not serve the law. I will be executed, but I will not plead guilty.

Moreover, I must point out that persecution against the Lord's church and against all Chinese people who believe in Jesus Christ is the most wicked and the most horrendous evil of Chinese society. This is not only a sin against Christians. It is also a sin against all non-Christians. For the government is brutally and ruthlessly threatening them and hindering them from coming to Jesus. There is no greater wickedness in the world than this.

If this regime is one day overthrown by God, it will be for no oth-er reason than God's righteous punishment and revenge for this evil. For on earth, there has only ever been a thousand-year church. There has never been a thousand-year government. There is only eternal faith. There is no eternal power.

Those who lock me up will one day be locked up by angels. Those who interrogate me will finally be questioned and judged by Christ. When I think of this, the Lord fills me with a natural compassion and grief toward those who are attempting to and actively imprisoning me. Pray that the Lord would use me, that he would grant me patience and wisdom, that I might take the gospel to them.

Separate me from my wife and children, ruin my reputation, destroy my life and my family — the authorities are capable of doing all of these things. However, no one in this world can force me to renounce my faith; no one can make me change my life; and no one can raise me from the dead.

And so, respectable officers, stop committing evil. This is not for my benefit but rather for yours and your children's. I plead earnestly with you to stay your hands, for why should you be willing to pay the price of eternal damnation in hell for the sake of a lowly sinner such as I?

Jesus is the Christ, son of the eternal, living God. He died for sinners and rose to life for us. He is my king and the king of the whole earth yesterday, today, and forever. I am his servant, and I am imprisoned because of this. I will resist in meekness those who resist God, and I will joyfully violate all laws that violate God's laws.

First draft on September 21st, 2018; revised on October 4th. To be published by the church after 48 hours of detention.

APPENDIX: WHAT CONSTITUTES FAITHFUL DISOBEDIENCE

I firmly believe that the Bible has not given any branch of any government the authority to run the church or to interfere with the faith of Christians. Therefore, the Bible demands that I, through peaceable means, in meek resistance and active forbearance, filled with joy, resist all administrative policies and legal measures that oppress the church and interfere with the faith of Christians.

I firmly believe this is a spiritual act of disobedience. In modern authoritarian regimes that persecute the church and oppose the gospel, spiritual disobedience is an inevitable part of the gospel movement.

I firmly believe that spiritual disobedience is an act of the last times; it is a witness to God's eternal kingdom and the temporal kingdom of sin and evil. Disobedient Christians follow the example of the crucified Christ by walking the path of the cross. Peaceful disobedience is the way in which we love the world as well as the way in which we avoid becoming part of the world.

I firmly believe that in carrying out spiritual disobedience, the Bible demands me to rely on the grace and resurrection power of Christ, and that I must respect and not overstep two boundaries.

The first boundary is that of the heart. Love toward the soul, and not hatred toward the body, is the motivation of spiritual disobedience. Transformation of the soul, and not the changing of circumstances, is the aim of spiritual disobedience. At any time, if external oppression and violence rob me of inner peace and endurance, so that my heart begins to breed hatred and bitterness toward those who persecute the church and abuse Christians, then spiritual disobedience fails at that point.

The second boundary is that of behavior. The gospel demands that disobedience of faith must be non-violent. The mystery of the gospel lies in actively suffering, even being willing to endure unrighteous punishment, as a substitute for physical resistance. Peaceful disobedience is the result of love and forgiveness. The cross means being willing to suffer when one does not have to suffer. For Christ had limitless ability to fight back, yet he endured all of the humility and hurt. The way that Christ resisted the world that resisted him was by extending an olive branch of peace on the cross to the world that cruci-fied him.

I firmly believe that Christ has called me to carry out this faithful disobedience through a life of service, under this regime that opposes the gospel and persecutes the church. This is the means by which I preach the gospel, and it is the mystery of the gospel which I preach.

The Lord's servant,

Wang Yi

I wept reading this most precious letter from a godly, persecuted saint. Hang on to this letter, beloved. It will greatly encourage you against a time to come, stir you to pray for the persecuted saints, and it will help you to remain faithful to the Lord in the years ahead.

CHAPTER 29

THE CONDITIONS ARE RIPE FOR A SPIRITUAL HURRICANE

There were 400 years of near silence from the days of the prophet Malachi until John the Baptist and Jesus came on the scene. No prophet had spoken. We don't have Biblical record of any prophetic vision or revelation. There was a famine of the true word of the Lord.

The old man Simeon and the old prophetess Anna were two of the faithful remnant who held on to the delayed promise of the coming Messiah and the consolation of Israel (Lk. 2:25-38). The ceremonial priestly sacrifices, the temple offerings, and the Sabbath rituals without the prophets speaking had created a great, lifeless vacuum among the Jewish people.

But in spite of outward circumstances and centuries of a divine pause, God's plan was still in motion and so much greater than they ever imagined. It not only included redemption for Israel but for the Gentile nations as well. The vacuum of the human heart would be filled to overflowing with new light and new life. The glory of God was on the horizon.

"In Him was life, and the life was the light of men" (John 1:4).

Herein we must understand what I call the principle of the vacuum. When a people are denied and deprived of the life-giving word and power of God for so long, it feeds the desire and hunger for it all the more. When the reality of God is taken from a people, the craving and panting in their hearts increases. When a society infiltrates our educational system from kindergarten to our universities with human-istic ideologies, with marxist socialism, with anti-Christ and anti-Semitic literature, with hatred, violence, and sexual perversion, the human heart begins to long for a purity from a more innocent time. The glory of Christ becomes the end of their search.

'*And the Word became flesh and dwelt among us, and we beheld His glory...*"(John 1:14).

Though Christ came 2000 years ago, there are still many nations who've been deprived of His gospel and His glory. Anti-Christ governments and religious regimes block the flow of God's blessings to a nation. They shut off the spigot, so that the water of life cannot get to the people.

But how do you shut off the hunger of a human heart? The potential of life flow into that vacuum is enormous. Here is the principle:

"*But where sin abounded, grace abounded much more...*" (Rom. 5:20b).

This principle is evidenced when scientists and meteorologists gauge the force of hurricane winds and water surges by the low-pressure systems that form over the ocean of a developing storm. There's a vacuum effect created that determines the violence of the winds. Such is the mystery of a human heart and a society that has been denied true spiritual light and life for so long.

In the last chapter, you read of this principle at work in China. In spite of an evil communist regime suppressing the people under an atheistic form of government, the Chinese church is flourishing. I'll never forget the image I saw not too long ago of a container of Bibles being opened and the Chinese recipients of those Bibles weeping with joy and scrambling to get their copy. The nation's outlawing of the Bible created a great vacuum in the heart of the people and producing a ravenous hunger for the written Word of God.

Iran, as a nation, is another recent glaring example. The Islamic regime there has starved their people of the gospel and reality of Jesus Christ for a long time. Yet now within that nation is one of the fastest-growing underground churches in the world. What happened? When you saturate a people with enough hate, strife, violence, and a dead, joyless religion devoid of God's love that produces no true peace because it contains no assurance of salvation, then you create a great vacuum and a hunger in the human heart to be filled with the reality of the true and living God.

When secularists attempt to create a post-Christian America, they actually create a hunger in people for sacredness. When atheistic university professors seek to erase our Judeo-Christian heritage, they actually create space for a new script of faith in God to be written in the human heart. What they are ignorantly doing is playing right into the devil's hand.

Satan has been overplaying his hand since Calvary. What he thought was the ultimate defeat turned into the greatest victory in the history of the human race. He is repeating this strategy in his plans to destroy America. All he is doing is adding to the increase of the groaning of creation to be delivered from the bondage of corruption.

The deeper our society sinks into hopelessness and despair, the greater the cry is for a living hope and eternal joy. The deeper the bondage of sin, and addiction to drugs, and sexual perversion, the greater the cry is for deliverance and freedom. This effect is happening in America right now, and globally as well. The earth is groaning for the manifestation of the sons of God (Rom. 8:22).

I propose to you that we are on the precipice of the greatest move of God and awakening that America and the nations have ever seen. I propose to you that, since the time of Christ and the early Church, we've not seen a move of God that comes close to the finale of what has been in God's heart from the beginning.

THE BEST IS YET TO COME

The days we are in remind me of the days of Haggai the prophet. There was great opposition to the work of God and rebuilding the temple. There was indifference and discouragement among the people. But the Lord stirred up His leaders and people to finish His work and promised the future would be more glorious than the past.

"So the Lord stirred up the spirit of Zerubbabel the son of Shealtiel, governor of Judah, and the spirit of Joshua the son of Jehozadak, the high priest, and the spirit of all the remnant of the people; and they came and worked on the house of the Lord of hosts, their God" (Hag. 1:14).

To every struggling pastor, I would like to say: Don't give up, and don't quit. Keep building the house of the Lord. Don't focus on church growth-ism, buildings, or money. Continually deflect all those cares to the Lord. Keep worshipping God and praying in the Spirit. Cultivate a positive outlook from the Word of God. Stop the criticism. Stop the complaining. Stop looking back on the "good ole days" when God was moving. Stop feeling crushed every time opposition comes. Instead, realize that God is stirring His leaders and His people as He did in the days of Haggai.

He is stirring them to keep building, keep loving, keep forgiving, keep praying, and keep believing. Stop thinking that America is too far gone, that our youth are too far lost and indifferent, and that there is no hope. Stop focusing on the anti-Christ spirit in our godless culture and what the devil is doing. Do not look to the temporal — look to the eternal. No matter what happens, the God of the truly righteous always wins.

"...we do not look at the things which are seen, but at the things which are not seen" (2 Cor. 4:18).

Faith sees the invisible and believes the impossible. The reason the people of God believe what He has spoken is that they have a different spirit.

Joshua and Caleb had a different spirit. They saw the same giants as the other spies, but they saw an even more gigantic God. But the majority couldn't see God in it, and so their unbelief kept them from entering into the promised land. They forfeited their future. No tears, no prayers, no sacrifices, and no human effort would ever allow them into the place God had originally prepared for them. They would wander 40 years in circles with the knowledge that they had rejected God and His promises.

I believe this is what's at stake at this critical juncture in our nation's history. An entire generation could forfeit their future if they do not follow the faith of their true spiritual forefathers.

Unbelief, murmuring, complaining, rejecting God's promises, rejecting God's leaders and those who preach the truth while listening to faithless liars, had caused an entire generation of Israelites to lose everything. Pastors and preachers who tell faithless lies from pulpits everywhere will have the blood of so many lost souls upon them.

THE FINAL HOPE FOR A FINAL MOVE OF GOD

In 1939, just before World War II broke out, Smith Wigglesworth told a young Lester Sumrall of three waves, representing different moves of God, that he saw later in the 1900s. The first wave he saw was the healing revival of the 1940s and '50s; then the second wave he saw was called "The Charismatic Renewal," which crossed denominational lines when multitudes received the baptism in the Holy Spirit. — Then

176

he saw a third wave of teaching on faith and healing that was labeled the "Word of Faith" movement.

But then, suddenly, he prophesied of one more wave. "After *that, after the third wave* (this one is still in the future at this writing)," he started sobbing.

"*I see the last-days revival that's going to usher in the precious fruit of the Earth. It will be the greatest revival this world has ever seen! It's going to be a wave of the gifts of the Spirit. The ministry gifts will be flowing on this planet Earth. I see hospitals being emptied out, and they will bring the sick to churches where they allow the Holy Ghost to move.*"

This is the fourth wave he saw, which is still in the future, but I believe it is at the door. I believe this wave is higher and greater than all the other waves Wigglesworth saw put together. This could be the final wave that gathers the final harvest of souls. This could actually be the wave that takes us onto the shores of heaven. Hallelujah! Glory to God!

I also believe America will be a main participant in this final wave and the massive in-gathering of souls that still remains. Cheer up! God is not done with America. God is not done with His Church in America. I believe she will arise from the tumult of the 2020s and complete her destiny.